Anything You Can Do...
NEW SPORTS HEROES
FOR GIRLS

Fast Lane to Victory

The Story of Jenny Thompson

by Doreen and Michael Greenberg,
based on interviews with the athlete

Illustrations by Phil Velikan

Wish Publishing
Terre Haute, Indiana
www.wishpublishing.com

Fast Lane to Victory © 2001 Doreen and Michael Greenberg

LCCN: 00-107209

Book edited by Rick Frey
Proofread by Heather Lowhorn
Cover designed by Phil Velikan
Cover Photo provided by AP/WIDE WORLD PHOTOS

Printed in the United States of America
10 9 8 7 6 5 4 3 2 1

Published in the United States by
Wish Publishing
P.O. Box 10337
Terre Haute, IN 47801, USA
www.wishpublishing.com

Distributed in the United States by
Cardinal Publishers Group
Indianapolis, Indiana 46268

Acknowledgments

The lifelong dedication of Carole Oglesby, Mariah Burton Nelson and Donna Lopiano to the promotion of women in sport has inspired us to write the *Anything You Can Do...* series. We'd like to thank the Women's Sports Foundation for its support and in particular the efforts of Yolanda Jackson and Marj Snyder.

Deepest thanks go to Holly Kondras, our publisher, for sharing our enthusiasm to promote new heroes for young girls.

Special thanks to Coaches Mike Parratto and Richard Shoulberg for reminiscing with us about Jenny's life.

Heartfelt gratitude goes to Marjorie Wuestner for the example of her life-long dedication to girls' physical education.

We could not have accomplished this endeavor without the enthusiastic help of Jenny's agent, Sue Rodin.

We are indebted to Michael Cohen and Jordan Shapiro for their support and wisdom.

We are forever grateful to our beautiful daughters, Alice and Jane, for their patience, example, advice and love.

We have always marveled, along with everyone else, at the awe-inspiring achievements of Jackie Joyner-Kersee and Julie Foudy. We are very proud that their insightful comments are part of our series.

Above all, we must thank Jenny, the hero of this book. Her talent and perseverance make her an example to readers young and old.

Finally, we wish to acknowledge the young girls who run and swim and shoot baskets and fence and play tennis and kick soccer balls and water ski and hit softballs. You look to the athletes who came before you for your inspiration. We look to you for the future.

Any errors of fact or omission are solely the responsibility of the authors. Michael believes that the mistakes are due to Doreen, and Doreen believes that they must be Michael's fault.

Doreen & Michael Greenberg

"I think little girls need to have big girls to look up to!"

– Teresa Edwards, five-time Olympian
& professional basketball player

Contents

Dear Reader,

The story of Jenny Thompson is one of a series of exciting, true stories about female athletes. Jenny grew up in a working- class New England coastal town with a single mom and three older brothers. As her family struggled to make ends meet, Jenny found friendship, fame and success in the swimming pool. The family folklore maintains that Jenny could swim well before she could walk. This water baby went on to win eight Olympic gold medals and break world records. Jenny had to deal with some hardships, including wearing a brace for scoliosis and being teased about being so tall and strong. And she did it with her constant positive outlook and rugged determination to succeed. Jenny's story will inspire you with the knowledge that dreams really do come true.

Doreen & Michael Greenberg

Dear Parent and Teacher,

Jenny Thompson's story is one of true inspiration. We invite you to read along and discuss with the young reader the circumstances of Jenny's life. We know that participation in exercise and sports can bring many rewards to young girls including a higher sense of self-esteem and positive relationships with others. This is also an opportunity to engage in a discussion of those frustrations and anxieties that young athletes face at any level of competition.

We have attempted to raise some of the social and personal issues that girls and young women often confront everyday. You are an important part of the process. Explore together. Read together. Talk together. Possible discussion questions, issues, and resources can be found at the end of the book in the "Sports Talk" section. BEST OF ALL, Jenny's story is optimistic and enthralling and a lot of fun to read.

Doreen & Michael Greenberg

Preface

by Julie Foudy

When I was in elementary school, all of my brothers' friends called me "Jimmy" because I was such a tomboy. I loved watching football and playing touch football. I loved watching the Los Angeles Lakers basketball team — those guys were my heroes... Magic, Worthy and Kareem. I would watch them dunk the ball and block shots. I wanted to emulate them, but a five-foot-tall girl had a hard time dunking the ball. I didn't have a Mia Hamm to watch on television. I didn't have a Jennifer Azzi to watch in the WNBA. And for sure, I did not have a Women's World Cup Soccer to watch on TV.

One of the lasting images of the Women's World Cup will be all the little girls watching women performing great feats in front of great crowds — painted faces and all. My special memory is an image of the huge smiles on all those painted faces. A dream became a reality. These same little girls are now thinking, "Hey, if Mia, Michele and Julie can do it, I can do it." Now, they are not only dreaming about a World Cup Trophy or an Olympic medal, they are believing in it.

For this reason precisely, all of us on the U.S. National Soccer Team realize the importance of being role models. We cherish the fact that we truly can make a difference in the lives of these children. We see it every day in their eyes and on their faces. We tell them to watch, to learn, and most importantly, to believe. If we can do it — they can do it. The reaction we get from them says it all... a huge smile and a high five.

JULIE FOUDY was a member and co-captain of the U.S. National Team that won the 1999 Federation Internationale de Football (FIFA) Women's World Cup. An 11-year veteran of the team, Foudy earned a gold medal in 1998 at the Goodwill Games. Foudy also was a captain of the U.S. National Team that won a gold medal at the 1996 Olympic Games and competed for the United States in the 1995 FIFA Women's World Cup, in which her team finished third. Foudy was a four-time NCAA All-American at Stanford University and was voted Most Valuable Player in 1989, 1990 and 1991. She was also a finalist for the Hermann Trophy in 1991 and 1992. Foudy is currently the president-elect of the Women's Sports Foundation.

Introduction

by Jackie Joyner-Kersee

More than 25 years ago, the Women's Sports Foundation was founded to promote the lifelong participation of girls and women in sports and fitness. We have been very successful, and we have seen many changes over the years. At that time only one in 27 girls played sports; now it's one in three. And that's because more and more opportunities exist to be a female athlete and also to follow female sports heroes.

Even with thousands of girls attending World Cup Soccer or cheering on their favorite WNBA team, we still have a long way to go. We need to get the message out to more girls. We need to let every girl know how great it feels to play sports and how very important it is to her whole being. We still have too many 11- and 12-year-old girls dropping out of sports or never even having had the chance to play at all. In fact, if a girl does not participate in sports by age 10, there is a less than 10 percent chance that she will be participating when she is 25.

Research suggests that girls who participate in sports have a real advantage over girls who do not.

Girls active in sports are more likely to be successful in school, less likely to get involved with drugs, and less likely to have an unwanted pregnancy. Sport and exercise can help to keep girls healthy, both physically and emotionally. The girl who is athletic feels stronger, eats and sleeps better, is more self-confident, and generally feels more positive about her life.

For a very long time, boys have had unlimited resources, such as books, movies, and games about sports and their favorite sports legends. Sport is where boys have traditionally learned about achieving, goal-setting, team-work and the pursuit of excellence. Girls and women should have these skills, too. We need to establish a large-scale network of resources about girls' sports and female athletes.

And we need to give girls their own heroes. "Anything You Can Do..." is unprecedented in its concept of offering real stories of new heroes to young girls. These are the adventures of young girls, coming from different backgrounds, who go on to achieve excellence in sports.

This series can open a whole new world for young girls. These books will give young girls a chance to explore the biographies of elite female athletes and their early sport experiences. The common thread that runs through all of these stories is a strong one — of perseverance and desire. Yet, each story is unique. Some are famous; some are not. Although the young reader may not always recognize the name of every athlete in the series, she may very well recognize herself, her friends and her teammates in these stories.

Doreen and Michael Greenberg bring to this series a long dedication to providing positive sport experiences for girls. I like their philosophy that it is not as important for the young reader to come away with the name of the person who won the big championship or the winning score, as an understanding of what it means to be a female athlete.

And by including the unique "Sports Talk" section in each book, Doreen has the opportunity to use her expertise as a sport psychology consultant and researcher to discuss important issues with parents and teachers. These are issues distinctive to girls in sports, including competing with the boys, making sacrifices, dealing with coaches, anxieties about winning and losing, and concerns about body image.

I am delighted that these books deal with a young girl's introduction to sports, the highs and lows of training and competition, and the reactions of family and friends, both positive and negative. It is so important for all of us to understand the young athlete as a complete person.

Most of all, the books in this series are fun and exciting to read. They will inspire girls to follow their dreams — whatever they are.

JACKIE JOYNER-KERSEE was widely considered to be the best all-around female athlete in sports when she became the first woman to win back-to-back Olympic gold medals in the heptathlon at the 1988 and 1992 Olympic Games. The heptathlon is a grueling event in which athletes contest seven different events (100-meters, 100-meter hurdles, high jump, javelin, 200-meters, long jump and 800-meters) over the course of two days. A pulled hamstring forced her out of the heptathlon competition at the 1996 Olympic Games, but she came back to capture a bronze medal in the long jump. She also won a gold medal in the long jump at the 1988 Olympic Games, a silver medal in the heptathlon at the 1984 Olympic Games and a bronze in the long jump at the 1992 Olympic Games. She still holds the world record of 7,291 points in the heptathlon, which she set in 1988 at the Seoul Olympics.

Fast Lane to Victory

to Victory

The Story of Jenny Thompson

GERTRUDE EDERLE WAS BORN IN NEW YORK IN 1906. WHEN SHE WAS 12 YEARS OLD, SHE SET A WORLD RECORD FOR THE 880-YARD FREESTYLE SWIM. SHE WON OLYMPIC MEDALS AT THE 1924 OLYMPICS IN THE 100-METER FREESTYLE AND THE 4 X100 RELAY, BUT SHE WAS BEST KNOWN FOR

CHAMPIONS *of the* WATER

HER LONG-DISTANCE SWIMMING. IN 1926 SHE BECAME THE FIRST WOMAN TO SWIM THE ENGLISH CHANNEL. IT TOOK HER 14 1/2 HOURS TO SWIM FROM ENGLAND TO FRANCE — THE FASTEST TIME EVER.

1

Guppies

Dover, New Hampshire — July 30, 1999

The kids of the Seacoast Swimming Association gathered at the outdoor pool here in Guppey Park, right off Route 4, next to the ice-skating rink. They were really excited. They were here to meet their hometown hero, one of the greatest swimmers ever.

Her giant shadow looms over the Seacoast swimming pool. She is a household name in Dover. It is such an honor to swim in "her" pool, that the little kids whisper her name. And for good luck, the big kids jump up and touch her name on the sign over the front door of The Jenny Thompson Competition Pool. Nobody minds the fingerprints all over the sign — it's become a tradition.

Next to the pool, at Guppey Park, you can see the stage set up for the Annual Cochecho Arts Festival that lasts all summer long. Last night there was a brass band playing music. Tonight there will be a magic show. But the most exciting event was about to happen for these young swimmers.

It was late morning. The sun was trying to burn through a thin layer of low-lying clouds. The young swimmers couldn't stand still. They laughed and joked among themselves. A small freckle-faced boy grabbed someone's swim cap and tossed it to a tall skinny kid, who threw it over the fence.

"Hey, cut that out. Give me back my cap! Not fair!"

Jenny and her mom had just finished breakfast at Jake's Restaurant on Third Street in the center of town. The food at Jake's was always good, home-made and plentiful — just the way Jenny liked it. As Jenny and her mom talked about the day's event, Charlie, the owner, came over to greet them.

"No charge for you, no charge for Jenny," he said in a heavy accent. "Let me show you something." And he led them over to the far wall. There he pointed to a faded newspaper clipping of Jenny pictured at her first Olympics.

"God bless you. I follow everything you do. You make all of us in Dover so proud. You make America proud. God bless you." He gave Jenny a big hug. It made Jenny and her mom smile.

● ● ●

At the pool, someone spotted the famous Olympic swimmer. "There she is. There's Jenny Thompson!"

Jenny and her mom had just pulled up to the pool parking area and gotten out of the car. Jenny smiled to herself as she walked under the sign at the entrance to the pool area.

THE JENNY THOMPSON COMPETITION POOL

The mayor and the town council had honored Jenny in 1995 by renaming the local pool after her. Wow! She never got over the thrill of seeing that sign. This was the very same pool where, just a few years earlier, she had trained. People say you can't go home again. Sure you can. Jenny was back in Dover to visit with her mom and say hello to some old friends. Then it would be back to California to continue training for the upcoming Pan Pacific Games in Australia.

After a bit of good-natured pushing and shoving, the kids managed to form a line. All of them were anxious to meet Jenny. They held out their swim caps for Jenny to autograph.

The youngsters knew that Jenny had grown up right here in Dover. She had swum for the Seacoast Swimming Association and Dover High School teams. Most of them also knew that Jenny had set world records and had competed in two different Olympics in Barcelona, Spain, in 1992 and in Atlanta, Georgia, in 1996. Jenny had won five Olympic gold medals, more than any other United States female athlete at the Summer Olympic Games.

Some of the kids also knew that Jenny was still training hard and still competing. In fact, she was swimming some of her best times ever. Sports writers for the local paper, *The Daily Democrat*, were beginning to write about Jenny's chances of breaking one of the oldest and most difficult records in swimming history — Mary T. Meagher's 18-year-old record for the 100 meter butterfly.

"Hi, Jenny Thompson. My name is Karen. Would you sign my swim cap?"

"Sure, kiddo. How long have you been swimming?'

"I'm 10 years old. I've been swimming here for two years."

"What are your favorite events?" asked the champion.

"Oh, I'm a sprinter just like you, and I'm good at freestyle and butterfly. Just like you."

"That's terrific," said Jenny. "How often do you practice?"

"Five times a week. I train hard and try to work on my strokes, just like Coach Parratto says."

"Great!"

Jenny signed Karen's swim cap with the waterproof marker: *Best of luck to a future champion — Jenny Thompson.*

"Do you want to know the secret of swimming your best?"

"Sure," Karen said excitedly.

Jenny put a hand on each of Karen's shoulders and looked her right in the eyes.

"OK, then — never forget why you began swimming in the first place. Never forget to have fun."

"Thanks Jenny Thompson. OK, I never will forget." Karen ran off to show her friends the autographed swim cap and tell them about Jenny's secret advice. It was a secret she was happy to share with her swimming pals.

Jenny stretched out her arms. Slowly she bunched up the powerful muscles in her shoulders, neck and upper back and slowly she released the tension. She felt the dull ache beneath her shoulder blades that all competitive swimmers feel. Her short blond hair was still wet from an early-morning workout. The sun, which had burned through the clouds, felt good on her face. A light southeasterly breeze carried a hint of the Atlantic Ocean shore. Jenny breathed in deeply. It was nice to be home.

"Hello, Jenny Thompson."

Jenny looked down at the smallest young swimmer. She wore her Speedo swim suit and goggles and swim cap and looked like she was ready to race any minute.

"Hello, yourself." Jenny smiled. "What's your name? How old are you?""

"I'm Elizabeth and I'm 7 years old. Can I ask you something, Jenny Thompson?"

"Of course you can. Ask me anything you want."

"When you were little, did you swim at the Jenny Thompson Pool?"

Jenny smiled and then started to laugh.

"I sure did — only it wasn't called the Jenny Thompson Pool, way back then. It was called Guppey Pool."

Jenny looked up and saw her mother talking to a group of parents over by the starting blocks. Mrs. Thompson must have sensed that Jenny was looking her way. She looked up and for a moment their eyes met. Each gave the other a warm smile. Jenny knew she had her mom to thank for the great success she enjoyed. She knew that Margrid Thompson had worked and sacrificed to raise Jenny and her three brothers, as a single mom.

Jenny also had a good idea what her mom was telling the parents of these young swimmers. She had heard the stories about a thousand times, of how Jenny could swim before she could walk. Jenny smiled to herself and went back to signing autographs.

On the way back to their house, Jenny and her mom passed the big wooden sign at the entrance to town. It was white with green lettering, and it read, "WELCOME TO DOVER — HOME OF OLYMPIAN JENNY THOMPSON." Jenny was amazed every time she saw the road sign. Margrid Thompson was always proud.

• • •

Georgetown, Massachusetts – 26 years earlier

It was the last weekend of August. Everyone at the pool was trying to squeeze the last bit of enjoyment from this New England summer day. In another week the pool would close for the season. In another month, the leaves on the trees would begin to turn bright yellows and reds, before crinkling up and falling to the ground.

Some boys were playing on the water slide. Again and again they would climb up the ladder and then slide down with a loud shriek, making the biggest splash they possibly could. Two little girls were tossing a big red and white beach ball. After a couple of throws, one of them would tip the ball into the pool.

"Hey, Mister, could you throw my ball back?" And the game would continue.

A group of old men were sitting at a table under a wide yellow beach umbrella. The men were playing cards. One old man wore a blue Boston Red Sox cap, and another was chewing on a big, fat, unlit cigar. No one had ever seen any of the card-playing old men actually swimming in the pool.

"Man on TV says to expect some rain."

"Rain?"

"That's right. Afternoon thunderstorms."

"Nah."

"Well, we'll see, won't we?"

10

All around the pool little kids were playing and young mothers were keeping a watchful eye on them, while gossiping with each other. Gradually, everyone's attention began to turn to the very remarkable scene in the middle of the pool.

A baby girl, only seven months old, was swimming with her mother and three brothers. She had the cutest round face with just a little blond fuzz on her head — like a baby duckling. She took to the water like a duckling, too. She would dip her head under the water and flap her arms and kick her feet. The baby in the little red swim suit with the white trim swam underwater from her mother to her 5-year-old brother Aaron. She swam from Aaron to her 8-year-old brother Erik, and from Erik to her 10-year-old brother Kris — and then back to her mom. Each time she would take in a big breath before going under water again. Then Mom would hold her high in the air, and the little baby girl would laugh and laugh.

Now, just about everyone at the summer swim club was watching.

"Well, I never... " someone remarked.

"It's the Thompson baby," someone else said. "Never saw anything quite like it before."

"Keep your eye on that one. I expect we'll be seeing her in the Olympics some day."

One by one, everyone went back to what they were doing — to the water slide, to the ball tossing, to the

card game. High in the western sky a line of thunderstorms was beginning to form. In the pool, little Jenny Thompson, her mother, and three brothers continued to splash and laugh and play.

• • •

It was still dark outside. The only sound in the big old house on Tenney Street was the soft flip-flop of her slippers as Margrid Thompson shuffled down the hallway past the rooms of her sleeping children. She stopped just outside her daughter's room and peeked inside. Jenny was such an angel – 6 years old, blond hair and blue eyes, cute as could be.

Jenny was sleeping in her white bed all bundled up in the pink afghan with white stripes that her grandmother had made for her. The room was pink and purple with pretty flowered wallpaper. In a white, wicker doll crib were lots and lots of Barbie dolls — Birthday Barbie, Malibu Barbie, Ken and Skipper, all with homemade outfits. Margrid Thompson looked again at her little girl. She smiled and shook her head. She wished that she had more time to spend with Jenny and her boys.

Margrid made herself a pot of coffee at the stove. She pulled her robe tightly around her. Although it was still August, the mornings in New England were already turning cool. She sipped from her mug and looked out the window as the clouds in the eastern sky began to turn pink. It would be another long and busy day. She wasn't complaining, though. It's just that she wished... well, anyway. She liked her job as a medical technologist at the hospital. There were tests to perform, lab reports to write up, and filing to get done. If only the budget wasn't so tight.

Kris wanted that new backpack. Erik and Aaron needed new shoes, and Jenny was starting first grade in a few weeks. She would need new everything. Margrid hoped that the car would hold up. It was making that funny sound now every time she started it. She would have to take it over to the garage after work and let the new mechanic take a look. Margrid knew that the Thompson family could be tough when they had to be. They'd all pull together. They would do just fine.

Oh, well. She'd just have time for a quick shower and then make breakfast for Aaron and Jenny. Kris and Erik were already out the door at their summer landscaping jobs. She decided to make French toast this morning. It was Jenny's favorite.

"Aaron! Breakfast! Wash up and get your sister."

"I'm already up, Mom," said a little voice from the top of the stairs. "I brushed my teeth and everything."

"Who's that?" asked Mrs. Thompson.

"Mom, it's Jenny."

"Jenny who?"

"Jenny Thompson!"

"Oh, that Jenny."

Mrs. Thompson smiled to herself as she cut big slices of crusty, fresh bread. She dipped each slice into the special egg batter, first one side and then the other. Then she carefully cooked the battered bread in the hot butter sizzling in the big iron skillet. Mmmm... it smelled good.

"Aaron, pour your sister a glass of milk, please."

"Mom, I'm 6 years old; I can do it by myself."

"Okay, sweetheart. But use two hands. Very carefully."

Aaron poured the dark, thick, maple syrup all over his French toast. His little sister took the syrup pitcher and did the same thing.

"Mom, this is really good," said Aaron, his mouth full of toast and syrup.

"Yeah, Mom... it's really good. Thanks," said Jenny.

"Kids, I may be a little late picking you up at Cederdale, today. I have to get the car checked out."

"No problem, Mom," said Aaron, licking the sticky maple syrup from his fingers. "We'll be sitting down by the front gate, under the trees."

"Yeah, no problem," agreed Jenny.

Mrs. Thompson dropped off Aaron and Jenny at the bottom of the gravel drive leading up to Cederdale.

"Jenny, do you have your swimsuit and your towel?"

"Sure do."

"Aaron, keep an eye on your sister for me."

"I'll keep my eye on Aaron, too, Mom."

"Good girl. Remember I'll be a little late picking you guys up this afternoon."

"I'm keeping my eye on Jenny," said Aaron with a mischievous smile. He pretended to pop out his eye and stick it on his sister. Jenny tore out of the car and up the drive, shrieking and giggling. Aaron ran after Jenny, careful not to catch her.

"Aaron, close the car door, please," shouted Mrs. Thompson. But Aaron and Jenny were already through the gate into the swim club.

Margrid Thompson got out and shut the door of the car. She got back into the driver's seat and turned the ignition key. The car made a funny, grinding noise, but it would not start. Again, she pressed down the gas pedal and turned the key. Again, the engine would not start. Margrid Thompson shook her head. She bit down on her lower lip and closed her eyes. It was going to be one of those days.

● ● ●

Cederdale Swim and Tennis Club in Groveland, Massachusetts was near the Thompson home. It wasn't very fancy, but it was perfect for the Thompson kids. They could play sports all day — softball, basketball, ping pong, tennis and swimming.

Jenny spent a lot of time in the pool, and she would always watch the older kids practice on the swim team. They wore matching swimsuits, and they sang team cheers.

One day Aaron said to his little sister, "You love to swim. Why don't you try out for the team?"

"But I'm only seven. Don't you think I'm too young?"

"Nah,"said Aaron, "You're real good in the water. Give it a try."

So Jenny and Aaron went to the Cederdale coach and asked if she could try out for the swim team. He said, "Sure, let's see what you can do. Jenny, I would like you to swim two lengths of the pool. If you can dive in, I'd like to see that, too."

Jenny was excited. She stood at the edge and sort of flopped in and swam to the other side and all the way back. She was out of breath but happy that she could do it.

When she got out of the pool, the coach came over and leaned down to her. She could tell by the look on his face that he wasn't going to put her on the team.

"Jenny, that was really good, but it looks like you haven't really had swim lessons. You don't know how to breathe the right way, yet. It's important to know how to breathe right for swimming. Maybe next year."

Jenny and Aaron walked away. With sadness in her voice, she asked Aaron, "What's wrong with the way I breathe? I got to the other end of the pool, didn't I ?"

Aaron answered, " I think it's because you need to be able to swim without getting out of breath. When you breathe the right way, you can go faster and swim longer."

"Can you show me how to do it, Aaron? Pleeeeease!"

"OK, we will work on it a little every day. The first thing you have to do is concentrate on blowing the air out, in the water, real hard. Like this."

Aaron took a deep breath and let it out with a *wooooh* sound. "In the water, you can see the bubbles. And let all the air out — like you are emptying all your breath."

Jenny practiced her breathing every day for the rest of the summer.

• • •

Trrriiillll!! Trrriiillll!! Trrriiillll!! The assistant swim coach at the Cederdale pool gave three loud blasts on the big sliver whistle that hung around his neck. "Let's go! Time trials. All swimmers in two straight lines."

Jenny knew that all the kids on the team were to race in pairs from one end of the pool to the other, turn quickly, and race all the way back to the start. Jenny loved being in the water. She loved swimming around, playing water tag with the other kids and diving for pennies on the bottom. But this racing stuff was new, and she felt a little nervous about it.

Jenny didn't really know if she was a fast swimmer or not. Last year, she couldn't even make the team. Maybe she should have watched closer when Aaron was practicing his racing dives. Some of the bigger kids could do special flip turns at the end of the pool, but Jenny didn't know how. Would the other kids laugh at her if she swam too slowly? Jenny got at the very end of one of the lines. She was hoping that her Mom would get there to pick her up before it was time for her to race.

The sun was now hiding behind some clouds. "Maybe it will rain," hoped Jenny.

The swim coach looked down at the list attached to the clipboard in his hand. "Jenny, you're next." He reset the big stopwatch he held in his other hand.

"C'mon Mom," prayed Jenny. She looked across the pool deck. The boy who was to race against Jenny was giving her a strange look. Jenny didn't know his name, but she knew he was one of the third graders and she knew that he had started in the year-round competitive swim program at the Danvers YMCA last year. She also knew that he had a big mouth and that he liked to tease the younger kids.

"Hey!" the boy shouted. "Do I have to race against a girl?"

The swim coach signaled Jenny and the boy to take their places.

"What's wrong with swimming with a girl? I swim with boys all the time," thought Jenny, although she

didn't say anything out loud.

"Swimmers — take your mark!" shouted the coach. *"Trrriiillll!"*

Jenny watched as the boy did a nice racing dive into the water. He extended his arms and sprung up and out with his feet. Jenny tried to copy him, but in her excitement she looked up too soon and *SPLAT!* She did a big belly flop. She took a big breath and saw the third-grader already several strokes ahead of her.

Jenny began to kick wildly and pull her arms through the water. "What would Mom say?" Jenny asked herself, as she struggled to get her arms and legs to move together. Mom would say, "Jenny Thompson, calm yourself down. Just do the best you can. That's all anybody can ever do." Jenny's breathing became easier and more regular. Now, with long arm strokes and strong kicks she was going smoothly through the water.

By the time Jenny had reached the far end of the pool, she was almost even with the other swimmer. She reached out and grabbed the edge of the pool. She turned and pushed off with her feet as hard as she could. Jenny was swimming so naturally. This was fun. Jenny forgot about the boy who was now struggling to catch up with her. She forgot about the other kids who were watching from the side of the pool. She forgot about the coach who was standing at the end of the pool holding out his big stopwatch.

Before she knew it, Jenny had touched the edge of the pool. Smiling, she looked up and saw the coach staring at her and then at the stopwatch in amazement.

"Whew! That was neat!" shouted Jenny. "Did I do OK?"

The third-grade boy finally finished. His face was red, and he was gasping for air. The coach looked at the boy, he looked at Jenny, and he looked again at the numbers on his watch. "Yeah, Jenny, you did OK. You sure did do OK."

DAWN FRASER STARTED SWIMMING TO HELP HER ASTHMA AND BECAME THE FIRST WOMAN TO WIN FOUR OLYMPIC GOLD MEDALS. SHE WON THE 100-METER FREESTYLE IN THE 1956 OLYMPICS AND THEN AGAIN IN THE 1960 AND 1964 OLYMPICS. SHE WAS ALSO THE FIRST WOMAN TO SWIM THE CHAMPIONS of the WATER 100 FREE IN UNDER 60 SECONDS. ALL TOGETHER, SHE WON EIGHT OLYMPIC MEDALS AND SET 39 WORLD RECORDS.

2

Wonder Woman

The changing colors of the fall leaves are brilliant. In New England, it is what is called "leaf-peeping time." The autumn has been mild and sunny with cool evenings. There hasn't been any frost yet, so the leaves have had a chance to change from green to vibrant shades of yellow, red, and orange.

Kids all over Georgetown are planning their costumes for Halloween. "Wonder Woman" has always been Jenny's favorite television show. Jenny loves Wonder Woman because she is so strong and powerful, and she is not afraid of anything. She is a great superhero with superhuman powers who became Wonder Woman by winning a contest to see who would be the champion of all the Amazon women. When Wonder Woman needs her powers, she spins around in a swirling flash of light and becomes the Amazon princess of power.

There was one particular episode Jenny remembers really liking. All these terrific athletes were being kidnapped by a madman who wanted them to compete in the Olympics for his imaginary country

Mariposalia which means land of the butterflies. Wonder Woman rescued them all.

Jenny is spinning around the living room in an imaginary flash of light. She is all excited. She wants to be Wonder Woman for Halloween. She has it all planned. She'll be dressed in red, white and blue. She will wear her red tights. She can make wide bracelets out of aluminum foil and wear them on her arms and pretend that they are bullet proof. She and her mom can make a headband with a red star on it. Her rubber rain boots will do just fine as Wonder Woman's boots.

Eight-year-old Jenny wants to wear her special Speedo swimsuit as her costume. She tells her mom that they can put an eagle on the front and some stars and stripes on the bottom to look like Wonder Woman's outfit. Jenny got this suit by making her first real swim team this year. But it's cold out in Massachusetts on October 31st, and Jenny's mom wants her to wear a sweater and a coat.

Jenny is running through the house in her Halloween costume. Around and around the kitchen table she goes, out into the front hall and up the stairs. In her imagination, she is moving so fast that she has become a red, white, and blue whirling blur.

She runs into Aaron's room and comes to a stop at the foot of his bed. Aaron is lying there, listening to the radio, his school-books spread out on the bed beside him.

"Who are you supposed to be?" he asks sarcastically. Jenny puts her hands on her hips, juts out her chin, and sings as loud as she possibly can:

Wonder Woman!
All the world is waiting for you
And the power you possess
In your satin tights
Fighting for your rights
And the old red, white and blue.
Wonder Woman!
Wonder Woman!
You're a wonder,
Wonder Woman!

Aaron is staring at his sister in amazement.

"Funny," he says, "you don't look like Wonder Woman. You look like my silly little sister, Jenny Thompson."

And with that, Aaron snatches his pillow from behind his head and hurls it at Jenny. Jenny ducks, turns, and runs screaming down the stairs.

Wonder Woman!
All the world is waiting for you...

• • •

It was so cool. Jenny was now part of the team. Her Danvers YMCA Dolphins swimsuit was a little big — but it was the last one they had, and it really didn't matter. She loved carrying her own swim bag

28

to practice. She had her special towel, her rubber pool shoes, her cap and her new goggles. She was now swimming every afternoon after school, and she had to protect her eyes from the pool chemicals. Besides, she could see clearer in the water with the goggles on.

● ● ●

"Whew! This is really tough," thought Jenny. The Dolphins' coach was teaching the youngest swimmers on the team the butterfly stroke. It was difficult at first, and it took strength and concentration — and lots and lots of practice.

First, the coach had them practice the up and down dolphin kick. Holding on to a kickboard, they practiced kicking down from the hips, wavelike, with both legs together. When Jenny kicked down, her hips would rise up in the water. They were all practicing the kick up and down the pool.

Then the coach collected the kickboards and instructed the young swimmers to put together the leg, body and arm movements of the butterfly.

"As your hips go up, your hands go in the water. There is a special rhythm to this stroke. When you catch the rhythm, it will look and feel wonderful."

Jenny's outstretched arms entered the water shoulder-width apart. She swept her hands out and back with a powerful stroke. As her palms, facing backward, passed through the water close to her legs, she lifted her chin forward and out of the water, taking a big breath. Now, out of the water came her arms, elbows first, then her hands with the palms facing in. As she snapped her face back into the water, Jenny again stretched out her arms, like the wings of a butterfly.

The tricky part was working her legs together with her arms. Jenny was finding it difficult, and she was feeling frustrated. She asked the coach for help.

"Jenny, think of the kick as two beats — a wave through the water and a snap back down. A wave and a snap. A wave and a snap."

Up and back swam Jenny, one length of the pool and then another and another. Little by little, she felt her body moving gracefully like a rolling wave.

The coach was telling them to roll forward and slide through the water. "Keep the body rolling — don't let it go flat," he was shouting.

"Jenny, sweep your hands under your throat, with your elbows pointing out."

"Butt out! Butt out, Libby."

"Keep the rhythm going, folks. RHYTHM! RHYTHM!"

In the car on the way home, Jenny told her mom all about practice.

"It was really neat. I learned a new stroke. It's called the butterfly. Coach said if I practice every day, I can swim the 25-yard butterfly race at our first swim meet."

Mrs. Thompson looked at her exhausted young daughter and smiled. By the time she pulled up to the big, old yellow house on Tenney Street, Jenny was fast asleep.

• • •

"Jenny — Jenny — Jenny — THOMPSON — THOMPSON — THOMPSON."

Jenny was swimming her very first 25-yard butterfly race — one length of the pool — for the Danvers Dolphins. The Danvers Y swimmers compete against other Y swimmers from the Eastern Massachusetts area. She had been working hard at practice every day for weeks.

She stretched out her arms like the wings of a butterfly and remembered the coach's advice about the two-beat dolphin kick.

"A wave and a snap. A wave and a snap." Jenny repeated the words in a rhythm, making her legs move together like the fin of a big fish.

Now, as she raced through the water as fast as she possibly could and touched the end of the pool, she heard the voice of the announcer on the loud speaker calling out her name. The sound echoed off the tile walls and all around the pool deck.

"Jenny — Jenny — Jenny — THOMPSON — THOMPSON — THOMPSON."

"Oh, no! I must have DQed," thought Jenny upon hearing her name called out. "I guess I've been disqualified for not doing the stroke correctly."

"A NEW DISTRICT RECORD IN THE 25-YARD BUTTERFLY."

● ● ●

Mrs. Thompson and Jenny were in the kitchen getting dinner ready. Jenny's short blond hair was still wet from the swim meet and a quick locker room shower. It seemed that Jenny's hair was always wet these days. Around her neck she wore three green ribbons.

Mom was making her special lasagna that Jenny and the boys loved so much. Her secret recipe called for fresh herbs and spices, lots of ground meat, plenty of thick tomato sauce, and gobs of melted cheese. Margrid Thompson always made extra. The boys sure did like to eat and so did Jenny.

Jenny was a big help to her mom. She liked to set the places around the table and prepare the salad. She washed and peeled and sliced the cucumbers. She carefully cut the tomatoes into wedges. Slicing the onions made her eyes water. She drizzled the salad dressing over the lettuce and tossed everything in a big bowl with a wooden fork and spoon. "Plenty for everybody," Jenny thought. It made Jenny proud to help her mom around the house.

"You're very quiet this evening, young lady," said Mom. "Are you feeling all right. Are you tired from the swim meet?"

"No, not really... well, a little, but a good kind of tired. You know what I mean."

Mrs. Thompson smiled. "It's not easy, is it... practice every day, swim meets, dance lessons, keeping up with your schoolwork. Do you have much homework this weekend, sweetheart?"

"No, not too much, really. Erik said he would check over my math problems, and Aaron is going to test me on my spelling words. We're having a quiz on Monday."

Just then, Aaron walked into the kitchen. He opened the refrigerator door and poured himself a big glass of milk. Then he stuck his hand deep down in the cookie jar.

"Just one," said Mom. "Dinner's almost ready."

"Aw, Mom," complained Aaron.

Jenny saw Aaron pop one cookie into his mouth and quickly stash two more into his shirt pocket. She decided not to say anything about it.

"So," said Aaron, "How did my little sister the fish, do at the swim meet, today?" Aaron, of course saw the three green ribbons around Jenny's neck. He knew that green ribbons were given to the swimmer who finished fifth in the race.

"I'm a Danvers Dolphin, not a fish, and I did really good, today," said Jenny. "I got three firsts — in the 25-yard fly, the 25-yard freestyle and in my relay. Miriam and Libby did really good, too."

Aaron looked at Jenny and looked again at the

three green ribbons around her neck.

"Mom," challenged Aaron, "Jenny's making up stories."

"No, I'm not making up stories," insisted Jenny.

"Jenny, I see the green ribbons. I know you didn't place first in your races."

"Well, it just so happens, Mr. Cookie Snatcher, that I did finish first in my races. I just traded away my first-place blue ribbons for green ones, that's all."

Aaron was staring at his sister in disbelief with his mouth wide open.

"Why would anybody in their right mind ever trade a first-place blue ribbon for a fifth-place green one?"

"Well, it just so happens that green is my favorite color!"

Aaron trudged out of the kitchen shaking his head from side to side.

"I can't believe this," he muttered just loud enough for Jenny to hear. "What a doofus!"

"I am not a doofus. Mom, tell Aaron I'm not a doofus," Jenny shouted. "Mom, it's OK to trade blue ribbons for green ones, isn't it?"

"Of course, Jenny," said Mom. "After all, green is your favorite color."

Jenny felt better. Big brothers could be so dumb sometimes. They were good for helping with homework and sticking up for you at school, but sometimes... they just didn't understand. Jenny was glad

that she had her mom around when she really needed someone who understood her feelings.

● ● ●

Now that Jenny was part of the 10-and-unders group on the Danvers Y swim team, she would be swimming in 50-yard events. There were new things to learn, because now she had to swim two lengths of the pool in a race. Today they were working on new racing dives and learning flip turns.

The new coach had explained how important it was to get into the water correctly. Most of the kids had first learned kneeling dives. Now, they were practicing "grab starts" off the starting blocks. The starting blocks were nonslip, raised stands attached to the side of the pool. The top of it sloped down to help the swimmer dive off.

Jenny was picturing what the coach looked like when she showed them how to do the grab start. Then she tried to copy the picture in her mind. She stood on the block with her toes curled over the front edge. She remembered that the coach bent her body over and grabbed the edge of the starting block between her feet. Jenny imitated what the coach had done.

"This feels funny, " Jenny called out to the swimmer in the next lane over.

"I know," said the girl, "I can't figure out where my hands go."

Just then she heard Libby shout out, "Woops!" and looked over to see her falling into the water in front of her starting block. Everyone started giggling, including the coach.

"Come on, swimmers," the coach shouted. "Let's keep trying. Do not lean forward or backward. That's right."

"Where are we supposed to be looking?" asked Jenny, trying to keep her balance.

"Just look back between your legs."

The coach continued. "OK, when I say 'Go,' I want all of you to push off hard with your legs — as if you had a spring in them. Make sure that your head stays down, your arms stay straight out, and then stretch forward into the water."

Jenny pictured what she should do. Then the coach shouted "Go!" and Jenny pushed off and up and out into the water. As she entered the water, she could hear the coach yelling, "Extend those bodies — stretch it out."

"Good job, folks," said the coach. "Now we are going to work on flip turns." And for this, the coach got in the water.

"I need a guinea pig to demonstrate on. Miriam, come on over." Coach and Miriam stood in the water at the shallow end, about 5 feet from the end of the pool. Everyone had gathered around to watch.

"You have all seen the older swimmers doing these turns. I know that some of you have been trying to do them, too. It takes a lot of practice to get it right. Let's try a shoulder roll first."

The coach told Miriam to swim slowly to the end of the lane, as she walked along side of her. When the young swimmer got near the end, the coach helped push Miriam's shoulder down and under, and threw her legs over, making her flip. Miriam bounced up out of the water and said, "Wow, that was fun!"

"Let's try it again, back from the wall, and this time after I flip you, try to push off from the wall with your feet."

Miriam swam toward the wall and the coach again flipped her by pushing down on her shoulder. This time, the swimmer touched the wall with her feet and tried to give a little push.

"Good," said the coach, "The push will get stronger as you practice."

"OK — everyone back in the water. First, I want all of you to space yourselves apart. Now, everyone do three somersaults in the water."

Everyone was having a good time doing the somersaults under the water. There was a lot of splashing and laughing and noise. The coach signaled everyone to come over to the side of the pool.

"Everyone, please line up and face the end and back up about 5 feet. When you swim to the wall, lead with one arm — almost touching the wall. Then, start your somersault, keeping your chin down on your chest, and do a dolphin kick."

The coach watched carefully as her swimmers tried their best to imitate the powerful flip turns they had seen the senior swimmers doing. Most of them would need a lot of practice to get it right. She did notice, however, that Jenny Thompson was flipping her body and pushing off as naturally as could be.

• • •

"Omigosh, omigosh, omigosh!" Jenny was leaning over the sink in the locker room and staring at the 10-year-old girl in the mirror. "Omigosh, omigosh, omigosh!" Who was that person with the horrible green hair?

Jenny ran screaming, her Speedo still dripping wet, through the locker room and out the door into the hall — right into her coach.

"Jenny, what's the matter? Are you OK?"

"Coach, my hair!" shouted Jenny. "It's green."

The coach was biting his lip. He was trying very hard not to laugh.

"You're right, Jenny. You're hair is green, all right. I guess we poured a little too much chlorine into the pool this morning."

"But it will wash out, won't it?" pleaded Jenny.

"Oh sure, sure," soothed the coach. "Your green hair will be blond again in a couple of weeks."

"A couple of weeks!" shrieked Jenny. "Omigosh, omigosh, omigosh!"

• • •

The summers were the best, because Jenny got to spend all day, every day at Cederdale where everyone loved to be in the water, and she could swim and compete with her water friends all the time.

The summer of 1984 was very special. It was the first time Jenny paid any attention to the Olympic Games. Jenny was 11 and all the kids watched the Games at Cederdale on a big television. It was very exciting for a lot of reasons. The Olympic Games were being held in Los Angeles, California, so everyone was thrilled about the American athletes competing on their home turf. Jenny especially loved all the patriotic stuff. There were fans at every event waving U.S. flags and dressed in red, white and blue. Every time an American won first place in her sport, there was a special ceremony. The champion got to stand up higher than everyone else. A gold medal on a ribbon was hung around her neck, and they gave her a bouquet of beautiful flowers. Then they raised up the United States flag really high and played The Star-Spangled Banner. Because it was happening in California, most of the people knew the words and were singing along and cheering and waving U.S. flags.

The American athletes were winning a record number of gold medals. Jenny was just beginning to understand what it meant to train hard for your sport and become very tired and sore from training. She also knew what it meant to win. All the female athletes really held Jenny's attention. Evelyn Ashford won the gold medal in track and field's 100-meter dash to become the world's fastest woman. Jenny liked the way that sounded.

And Joan Benoit, who also lived in New England, became the first woman to win an Olympic women's marathon race. Joan was a familiar name because she had won the Boston Marathon. Everyone at Cederdale cheered as she came running through the tunnel and into the Olympic stadium with her white cap on her head. The television announcer told a story about how Joan Benoit started running because of her two older brothers, who were runners.

"That's over 26 miles," the TV announcer said. Jenny only liked the short races in the pool. She couldn't imagine racing for over two hours.

In gymnastics everyone was excited about Mary Lou Retton. The little girl was almost a foot shorter than Jenny, but she was so gutsy and powerful. She got the first perfect score of "10" in the gymnastic event called the vault, and she became the first American female to win an Olympic gold medal in gymnastics.

But most of all, Jenny was fascinated by the Olympic swimming competition. Those American women became her new heroes. She watched Tracey Caulkins, Tiffany Cohen and Dara Torres glide swiftly through the water to win their races. And Mary T. Meagher was just amazing. She won the gold medal in the 100-meter and 200 meter-butterfly events. And then she won a third gold medal as part of the four-person medley relay team. The man on the television told a story about how Mary became famous when she was just 14 years old. She was at an international swimming championship in Puerto Rico and broke the world record in the 200-meter butterfly race. Her friends always called her "Fishy," and she had a stuffed frog she called Bubbles.

But the best part was watching Nancy Hogshead and Carrie Steinseifer tie for the gold medal in the 100 free. It was really cool, thought Jenny, that they both got first place. The wondeful excitement surrounding the Olympics made quite an impression on an 11-year-old New England girl. Would she swim in the Olympics one day?

• • •

Jenny was looking out the window of the fast moving elevated train. She turned back to look at her mom, who was daydreaming, and then she looked at the subway map on the wall and tried to find the "red line" they were on. Mrs. Thompson and Jenny were taking the "T" to the medical building in Boston. Jenny's pediatrician had told Jenny's mom about a special doctor for her back problem.

42

After examining Jenny and looking at her x-rays, the doctor sat down to talk to them.

"See how Jenny looks like she is leaning to one side and one shoulder is higher than the other? Jenny has a moderate case of scoliosis," said the doctor. "It is a sideways curvature of the spine. It happens to many more girls than boys, and we notice it during the beginning of the teen years."

"What causes this?" Mrs. Thompson asked.

"We don't know why it happens. We just don't want it to get any worse. The best we can do to prevent that is for Jenny to wear a brace, like this one, here, for a couple of years. It will act as a support for her spine."

The doctor turned to Jenny and asked, "Jenny, do you have any questions?"

"Can I still be on the swim team? It is very important to me," Jenny said with a worried look on her face.

"Of course. As a matter of fact, exercise is very good for this condition. It helps to strengthen the muscles surrounding the spine."

"Do I have to wear that brace in the water?"

"No, of course not."

"What else do we need to do?" Mrs. Thompson asked the doctor.

"Jenny will need follow-up examinations and periodic X-rays. The brace treatment should do the trick."

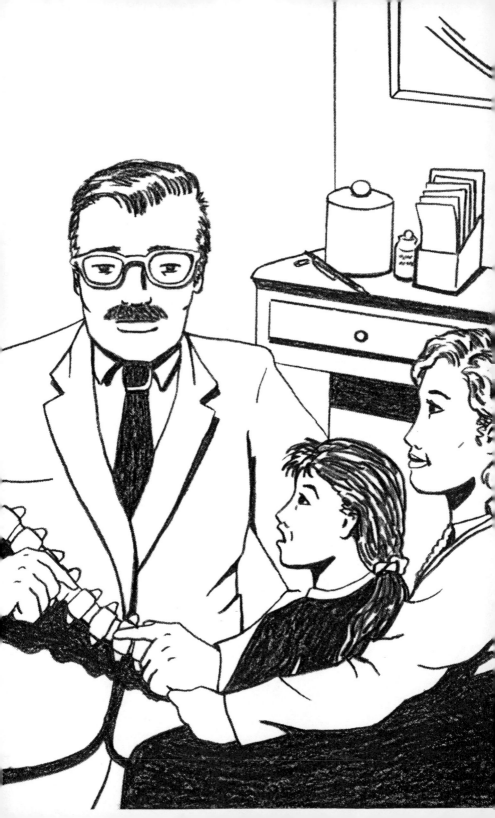

Jenny and her mom left the doctor's office and headed back to the "T" train. Jenny was very quiet. Mrs. Thompson put her arm around Jenny and said, "Let's go do some shopping. They have such nice stores here in Boston. We can find some pretty tops to cover the brace."

Jenny perked up a bit and said, "Sounds like a good idea, Mom."

• • •

Jenny was squirming about in her seat as her mom drove her home from dance class at the Joyce Dance Studio. She had been studying ballet, tap and jazz for the past six years. Mrs. Thompson could tell that her daughter had something on her mind. Soon, Jenny spoke up.

"Mom," said Jenny, "you know that I really like my dance classes and all."

"Of course, dear."

"I really like the instructors and the other kids."

"Yes, Jenny."

"It's just that no matter how hard I try and how much I practice, I never really think of myself as a dancer. Some of my friends, like Sarah Rice, just seem so much more natural and graceful than I do.

"But with swimming it's different. Even on my toughest days at the pool, if I'm not so fast, or if I don't feel so good, I always feel like I'm a swimmer. Does that make any sense?"

45

"It makes a lot of sense, Jenny."

"Whenever I'm at dance class, all I can think about is getting back in the pool. Mom, if I were to give up dance, would I be a quitter?"

"No, sweetheart, not at all. The Thompson women are not quitters. It's just that you're growing up, that's all."

Jenny stopped fidgeting about and turned to look at her mom.

"What do you mean?"

"Well, as you grow up you have to make decisions. You have to make choices that are not always easy. Deciding to give up dance to concentrate on swimming is a very hard choice. But I think that you are making the right choice."

"So you're not disappointed in me?" asked Jenny.

"No, darling. I'm very proud of you," replied her mom.

Jenny sat very still. She thought about what her mom was saying.

"Thanks, Mom," said Jenny.

Mrs. Thompson looked over at her daughter.

"Thanks for what?" asked her mom with a smile.

"Thanks for being my mom."

● ● ●

It was a sunny spring day and Jenny's sixth grade gym class was playing out on the athletic field. Jenny saw her friend Sue standing over by the soccer goal, talking and laughing. Jenny smiled and waved. She saw that Sue was with that mean boy who liked to make fun of everyone, teasing them and picking on them. As Jenny started to walk away, she heard the boy call out, "Hey, tomboy – show us your muscles!"

Jenny tried to ignore him. Sue and the boy were giggling and pointing right at her.

"There goes Too Tall Thompson," Jenny heard Sue say.

Before Jenny really knew what was happening, she and Sue were rolling on the ground — scratching, hitting, and pulling hair. The physical education teacher quickly ran over and broke up the fight.

"This is simply not acceptable behavior, young ladies." She grabbed both Jenny and Sue by the arms and marched them off to the principal's office.

That evening Jenny sat quietly at the dinner table. She didn't feel very hungry.

"Jenny," said her mom, "sometimes kids can be very cruel. They say some horrible, unkind things. In fact, sometimes grown-ups can say mean things, too."

"It's not that, Mom. If Sue wants to be that way, well, that's her business. I don't have to have anything to do with her."

"You're right dear, that's Sue's problem, not yours."

"But it is my problem. Don't you see? Sue's right. I am bigger than the other girls. I do have big muscles. And I do have braces on my teeth, and I have to wear that big ugly brace for my back!"

"But, Jenny..."

"Mom, please! Don't tell me any stories about ugly ducklings that someday turn into beautiful swans. That just doesn't make me feel any better at all."

Jenny ran out of the kitchen and up the stairs. Mrs. Thompson heard Jenny slam the door to her room. As she heard the muffled sobs from the top of the stairs, Jenny's mom sat at the kitchen table. She shut her tired eyes and bit down on her lower lip. It was very hard to see her child so unhappy.

DONNA DE VARONA WAS 13 YEARS OLD WHEN
SHE MADE HER FIRST OLYMPIC SWIM TEAM IN
1960. AT THE NEXT OLYMPICS IN 1964, SHE
WON TWO GOLD MEDALS, SETTING AN OLYMPIC
RECORD IN THE 400 INDIVIDUAL MEDLEY RACE
AND A WORLD RECORD
ON THE 4 X 100 FREE
RELAY TEAM. IN HER
SWIMMING CAREER, SHE
WON 37 NATIONAL TITLES. SHE BECAME THE
FIRST FEMALE SPORTS BROADCASTER ON NA-
TIONAL TELEVISION AND THE CO-FOUNDER OF
THE WOMEN'S SPORTS FOUNDATION.

3

Practice, Practice, Practice

Jenny Thompson made the turn and pushed toward the finish. With each powerful stroke, she became stronger and stronger. With each kick she went faster and faster. Thousands of onlookers cheered her on. Jenny glanced up and saw her three teammates in the 4 x 100 meter relay jumping up and down, shrieking wildly. A NEW WORLD RECORD. AN OLYMPIC GOLD MEDAL.

Jenny replayed the scene in her imagination again and again as she swam her practice laps. She loved swimming for her new team, the Seacoast Swimming Association, in Dover, New Hampshire. It was a long drive for Mom, 45 minutes up and back from Georgetown every day. Mom wanted her to be in the best program available. Coach Mike Parratto had come up from Boston the year before to take charge of the swim team at SSA.

Under Coach Parratto, practices were hard, but they were fun, too. Jenny knew that she was becoming a better swimmer. And she felt good about herself and proud of her accomplishments. At the beginning of the season, the coach had asked the young swimmers to write down their goals for the coming year.

"I want you to write down three goals — your dream goal, your goal for the season and your goal for this week," the coach told them. "Each week we will meet and go over your individual goals and see how it is going."

The coach continued, "Before you write anything down, I would like you to think about this. Your goals should be just that, your own — not what your parents want, not what other swimmers want, not even what you think your coaches want."

Jenny started thinking and dreaming. Then the coach said, "And make them believable — something you think you can really do." It was fun for Jenny to imagine her dream goal and season goal. It was harder to plan what she wanted to do this week. It made her focus on what she needed to work on right now. She was gaining confidence with each practice with Coach Parratto and his wife, Amy. They were both such good teachers and although they were tough, they were very kind, too.

At swim meets, if Jenny failed to make her time, or lost a race, the coach would just call it a "temporary nonsuccess." His first reaction was always, "Next time, this is what we do..." Jenny and Coach Parratto would work out a plan to improve the next performance.

For every swim practice, Margrid Thompson drove Jenny the 45 minutes it took to get to Dover, New Hampshire from their home in Massachusetts. Sometimes during practice, Mrs. Thompson would drive around town or get a cup of coffee. She liked Dover. It was an old New England town. There was a covered bridge over the Cochecho River. There were old lumber and grain mills and old federal style architecture.

The center of town was tree-lined and only a few streets wide. Central Avenue was full of colonial brick buildings over three hundred years old. The small village had a real community feeling. In the beginning of October, they were getting ready for the Apple Harvest Festival, setting up booths along Central Avenue for crafts and games. The more she came here, the more she liked it. And Jenny was really enjoying Seacoast Swimming and Coaches Mike and Amy.

"I have decided we should move to Dover, Jenny," her mom announced one day the following spring.

"But Mom," said Jenny, " it will take you so long to get to work."

● ● ●

One beautiful Saturday afternoon in late spring, Mike Parratto, the Seacoast swim coach, and his wife, Amy, were walking around Dover doing some weekend errands after practice. Amy had a few things to pick up at the market, and Mike wanted to stop at the hardware store to check out the power tools and the newest gadgets. They turned the corner and almost bumped right into Jenny Thompson.

"Hi, Coach Parratto. Hi, Mrs. Parratto," said Jenny.

"Hi yourself, Jenny, " said the coach.

"Watcha doing?" asked Amy Parratto.

"Oh, you know... nothing much. I'm just sort of hanging out. Some of my friends are inside buying ice-cream cones."

"Don't you want an ice-cream cone, too?" asked the coach.

"Well, I don't know... I guess it's getting kind of late and all."

"Jenny, if I treat you to a double-scoop cone, do you think that you'll be able to finish your dinner?"

"Oh, I'm a real good eater, Coach. It won't be any problem, at all."

Jenny gladly accepted a dollar and a half from her coach and hopped into the ice-cream store, turning to say, "Thanks a million, Coach."

"What was that all about?" Amy asked, turning to her husband. "Do you think we have a swimmer with an eating problem?"

"Jenny Thompson doesn't have an eating problem of any kind," replied Mike Parratto. "Jenny Thompson might just have an I-spent-all-my-allowance problem, that's all."

· · ·

Bryan Adams was playing on her tape machine. Jenny loved Bryan Adams — especially the song "Summer of '69." It was snowing again outside her window. It always seemed to be snowing in February. A lot of her swimming buddies were down in Florida for the Presidents' Day holiday break from school. In Florida, the swimmers were able to train in outdoor pools. Jenny turned from the window back to the book in her lap.

"What are you doing, sweetheart?" asked Jenny's mom as she passed her room.

"I'm reading that new book I got — about the Olympic swimmer from Australia."

"How is that book? Do you like it?"

"Yeah. Dawn Fraser is her name. She is pretty cool. She was a big deal in Australia — a three-time Olympic champion in the 100 freestyle. But she really liked to have fun and be a regular person."

"Glad you are enjoying your book, Jenny." Mrs. Thompson went downstairs to make some soup.

Jenny turned back to the story. She liked the part about Dawn Fraser being so nervous before an Olympic trials swim meet one day, that she forgot to put her swimsuit on under her warm-ups. As she started to lift off her jacket, the official shouted out to Dawn. He let her go back into the locker room and get her suit on.

It reminded Jenny of a nightmare she would have sometimes before a big race. But in her dream, Jenny would be standing there naked on the pool deck. Then everyone would notice and start to laugh, and she would run back into the locker room.

It was funny what being nervous sometimes did to her. She would get so worried about winning. Sometimes her mom would have to force Jenny to eat breakfast, because she would just feel sick to her stomach on the morning of a race. But once she got in the water, everything felt fine.

And even Dawn Fraser had scary dreams before big events. She wrote about them in the book. She even had them the night before winning her first gold medal. In Dawn's nightmare, she had honey on her feet, and she got stuck to the starting block.

Jenny thought about how Dawn Fraser had described winning that first Olympic gold medal in swimming. She had said that it took less than a minute to win the Olympic 100-meter championship, and in that minute she became part of history.

"It can be the biggest, the loveliest, the most memorable minute of your life," wrote Dawn Fraser in her book, *Below the Surface: Confessions of an Olympic Champion.*

---

*Fraser, Dawn with Harry Gordon. *Below the Surface: Confessions of an Olympic Champion*. William Morrow & Company, 1965;   p. 84.

Jenny thought about those words. Would she ever experience an Olympic moment?

• • •

Jenny was so excited. Both she and her brother Aaron had qualified for the Junior Nationals swim competition. She was only 12 years old, and she would be swimming against many of the best young athletes in the whole country.

Jenny and Aaron piled into the back seat of Coach Parratto's old Datsun 210. The coach adjusted the rearview mirror and made himself comfortable in the driver's seat, while Amy Parratto folded and arranged the maps. Coach Parratto gave a brief *TOOT-TOOT* on the horn and shouted, "We're off!" as they all buckled-up their seat belts and drove out of Dover, New Hampshire. They would be driving all the way to Alabama.

A half-hour later, Aaron said that he was getting hungry, and Jenny said that she had to go to the bathroom. After a quick visit to the rest-stop and snack bar, they were back on the highway heading south along Interstate 95. With another quick *TOOT-TOOT* on the horn, the coach shouted, "We're off, AGAIN!"

"I have an idea," suggested Amy Parratto. "Let's play geography. I'll name a place, anywhere in the world. Then Jenny will name another place that starts with the last letter of the first place, OK? How about Barcelona?"

"OK," said Jenny, "Barcelona ends with an A, so I'll say Atlanta."

"Good," said Amy. "That's the idea. OK, Aaron, now it's your turn."

"All right, I'll go with Arkansas."

"Arkansas," repeated Jenny. "How is that spelled? Does it end with a *W* ?"

"W!" teased Aaron. "I can't believe you got an *A* in spelling. No, Arkansas, does not end with a *W*, it ends with an *S*."

"I knew that," scoffed Jenny. "I was just testing you, that's all."

"Oh, sure you were."

"Now kids," said Amy. "Come on now; we've got a long drive ahead of us."

"OK, my turn," said Jenny. "Let's see, I'll say Sydney."

"Cindy?" questioned Aaron. "There's no such place as *Cindy*."

"Not *Cindy*," answered Jenny. "SYDNEY — like in Sydney, Australia."

"Oh, that Sydney!"

"Only two more days to go," said Coach Parratto.

A few minutes later Jenny and Aaron were both sound asleep. When they woke up, they were already in New Jersey. Jenny decided to count all the red, white and blue cars on the New Jersey Turnpike. "There's one... there's another one."

"OK," said the coach. "Anybody hungry?"

"I could eat a burger," said Aaron.

"I could eat a burger, too," chimed in Jenny. "And some fries with lots of ketchup. And maybe an ice-cream cone."

After lunch, they crossed over the bridge into Delaware. Jenny decided to count cows. "There's one... there's one... there's another one..."

"OK," Aaron complained. "Coach, just let me out here. I'll walk to Alabama."

In Maryland, Jenny decided to count horses. "There's one... there's another one... "

"Maybe, I'll walk to Alabama, too!" muttered Coach Parratto.

"Now, now, Mike!" Amy warned her husband with a quick look.

In Virginia, Coach Parratto pulled into a little motel just off the highway. He climbed out of the Datsun and slowly stretched his arms and legs.

"Anybody hungry?" he asked with a yawn.

"I could eat a burger," said Aaron

"I could eat a burger, too," answered Jenny. "And some fries, and maybe for dessert..."

"An ice-cream cone!" shouted Coach Parratto, Amy and Aaron all at the same time.

The next morning, bright and early, they were back on the road again.

"I know," Amy suggested, trying to sound enthusiastic, "let's all sing some songs."

Coach Parratto started singing Bob Dylan's *Blow-*

ing in the Wind, but Amy said, "No way!" and Jenny said she didn't really know the words.

By the time they reached North Carolina, Jenny was singing a Billy Joel song:

> *What's the matter with the clothes I'm wearing?*
> *Can't you tell that your tie's too wide?...*
> *Everybody's talking 'bout the new sound*
> *Funny, but it's still rock and roll to me.*

At first, Aaron held his ears and made faces as Jenny sang, but in a little while, he was joining right in as they sang the last verse, laughing loudly –

> *It's the next phase, new wave, dance craze, anyways*
> *It's still rock and roll to me.*

In Georgia, they turned off Interstate 95 and headed west toward Alabama, at the Gulf of Mexico.

"All right," said Coach Parratto, "a quick stop for lunch. We've got a way to go before it turns dark."

When Jenny ordered her hamburger and fries in the roadside restaurant, the waitress asked her where she was from.

"You talk funny. You sure don't sound like y'all are from around here."

That afternoon, the coach started singing some folk songs in the car. At first, Amy, Aaron and Jenny all groaned and held their ears, but by the time they crossed the Georgia-Alabama border, all four were happily singing away:

This land is your land
This land in my land
From California, to the New York Island
From the redwood forests
to the gulf stream waters
This land is made for you and me

• • •

Jenny was going to swim the 50-meter freestyle race.

"There's no pressure on you, Jenny," said Coach Parratto. "You're only here for the experience and to have fun. They will take the top eight swimmers from the preliminaries for the finals. Don't worry. Most of these kids are older and have been here before."

Coach Parratto had gotten Jenny up at 6:00 that morning. They had gone over to the practice pool for a quick warm-up swim. Then, they had gone out for breakfast. Jenny had ordered only a slice of canteloupe.

Coach Parratto and his wife Amy watched as Jenny joked and giggled with the other swimmers. Then she took her place behind the starting block for her qualifying heat.

"Do you see what I'm seeing?" Amy asked her husband Mike. The laughing and silliness had disappeared. Jenny had somehow turned into a very serious and very determined young athlete. Very

calmly, Jenny stretched and adjusted her goggles. She got up on the starting block and looked straight down her lane. She wasn't paying any attention to the other swimmers on her left and her right. She seemed to be blocking out all the noise and nervous excitement from the spectators in the stands.

"Swimmers, take your mark!" They were off. Amy and Mike watched in amazement.

"How did this happen?" asked Amy as she watched Jenny swimming her best race ever.

"I don't know," said the Coach. "Do you think, maybe, it was all the hamburgers?"

"Maybe it was the ice cream," kidded Amy.

"It's probably just that she has such a great coach."

"That must be it," agreed Amy. "She's swimming so fast to get away from your singing."

Jenny finished seventh in the prelims and made the finals at her first Junior Nationals. In the finals, Jenny came in sixth place. She had qualified with a Senior National time. Jenny had discovered something very important about herself. Not only did she like to swim and compete, but she wanted to *win*.

● ● ●

The Seacoast Swimming Association team was in Cambridge, Massachusetts, to swim against their biggest rival, the Burnell Gators, a big city team from Boston. It was a two-day meet with prelims on Friday and finals and relays on Saturday. Most of

Jenny's teammates were staying overnight at the Charles Hotel in Cambridge. Jenny was a little disappointed when her mom said that they would have to drive home to Dover on Friday evening and then drive all the way back down to Cambridge early on Saturday morning.

"But, Mom," Jenny began to complain. "All the other kids..."

"None of that, please, young lady," said Mrs. Thompson. "This is just the way it is, that's all. This is just the way it has to be."

Of course, Jenny knew that money was always a little short. Mom had to pay dues for Jenny to belong to Seacoast, and with travel expenses to swim meets and all of the other household costs, the Thompson family kept to a very tight budget.

"That's just the way it has to be," Jenny would hear her mom say again and again.

Seacoast won the meet. Coach Parratto and his young swimmers triumphed over the much bigger Boston team. Jenny and her friend Larissa were the stars. Jenny won the butterfly, freestyle and individual medley, with Larissa a very close second. Larissa won the backstroke, with Jenny coming in at number two. Together, they helped Seacoast take almost every relay event from the Gators.

The kids were happy and excited as they left the locker room and poured out into the bright autumn sunshine. They hugged each other and slapped high-fives, proud of their big win.

"Mom, Allison and Larissa are going out to lunch with their parents to celebrate. Can we go with them?"

"I'm afraid we won't be able to join them, sweetheart. But I did pack a special lunch for the two of us, and we could have ourselves a little picnic. You'll see — it will be fun."

Jenny turned away and trudged down the street. "It's not fair," she muttered . "It's just not fair."

Jenny angrily marched two or three steps in front of her mother, kicking up the fallen leaves as she went. Finally, she stopped and turned and looked down at the ground.

"I'm sorry, Mom," Jenny said softly.

"I know, dear," said her mom, putting her arms around her daughter.

Hand in hand, Jenny and her mother walked toward the Charles River. They walked through Harvard Yard, with its old red-brick buildings all around them. Students from Harvard University were playing touch football, tossing frisbees, or just sitting and reading in the afternoon sun.

They walked along the grassy river bank and out onto the Weeks Footbridge. Jenny stared down at the dark water flowing slowly beneath them. She saw rowers in their racing sculls, rhythmically stroking the water with their oars. She stared up at the sky and saw the wispy white clouds floating above.

"Mom, are we poor?" asked Jenny.

Mrs. Thompson turned to her daughter. "No, Jenny, we are not poor, but we are a long way from being rich. We have enough money to eat plenty of good, healthy food and live in a nice, warm house. But, I'm afraid, we don't have nearly enough for expensive hotels and restaurants. That's just the way it is."

"I know Mom, and I understand, really."

"You know Jenny, people can be rich in other ways, besides just having a lot of money."

"What do you mean?"

"Well, people can be rich in talent or imagination, or people can live a life rich with friends and wonderful experiences."

Jenny thought about what her mother was saying.

"Can people be rich with love?" asked Jenny.

"Yes, of course, darling."

"Mom, I think that I must be one of the richest people in the whole wide world."

"Oh, Jenny," said Mrs. Thompson as she hugged her daughter.

"Hey," said Jenny, "didn't you say something about a delicious lunch?"

"I sure did. I made you some liverwurst sandwiches with mustard on crusty round rolls."

"Oh, Mom," said Jenny. "You used to make that for me when I was a little girl."

"You're still my little girl, Jenny. You'll always be my little girl, no matter how big you get."

● ● ●

Coach Parratto used a lot of dry-land training as part of his workouts.

The team had to share pool time with other community swimmers, so he and Amy designed some tough workouts out of the pool to keep the swimmers in good shape and to give them more power in the pool.

Everyone was doing sit-ups with partners. With legs bent at the knees, Jenny did sit-up after sit-up while another swimmer held her feet. Then they switched places.

"OK, folks, time for towel exercises," shouted Amy. "Let's do shoulder lifts first."

Jenny and her partner grabbed a towel. Jenny held the towel with both hands at chest level, while her partner kneeled down and held the towel with all her might. Jenny then tried to lift her arms, with her elbows bent out — trying to lift the towel with her shoulder power while the other swimmer pulled down.

"Now let's do curls!" ordered Amy.

Holding the towel at waist height, with palm facing up, Jenny pulled up on the towel, bending her arms at the elbows. Her partner pulled the towel downward. Jenny continued curling and tightening the muscles in her upper forearms. Then they switched places.

"Towels down. Let's switch to surgical tubing and triceps exercises," Amy announced.

Surgical tubing was like a giant rubber band. It was tough work, but it was fun, too. Jenny hooked it around one of the metal stands for the bleachers and started her triceps extension exercise. Facing the bleacher, with her legs slightly bent, Jenny pulled the tubing with each hand and extended her arms back behind her. You had to be careful when you stopped and let go, so it didn't bounce back.

"Time for stretches now," called out Amy.

• • •

Dick Shoulberg, from the Foxcatcher Swim Team in Pennsylvania, was named the head coach for the United States team going to the Pan-Pacific championships. He wanted Jenny Thompson on the 1989 team. Shoulberg knew about Jenny from his friend, Mike Parratto, and she was already getting a fine national reputation. She was a first-time member of the U.S. National Team when she was 14 years old. Jenny made the finals for the 50-meter freestyle at the 1988 Olympic trials and almost made the Olympic team when she was only 15.

Being part of the prestigious Pan-Pacs team and going to the international event in Tokyo, Japan, was very exciting for 16-year-old Jenny. And getting a chance to swim for Shoulberg would be an experience! Jenny had always heard so much about him.

69

His swimmers would always complain about his long distance workouts, but they loved their coach.

The first thing Coach Shoulberg did was ask each of them to tell him something unique about themselves. The swimmers were mostly from California and Texas and Florida. So when he got to Jenny, she said, "I have a cross-country skiing trail in my backyard and a red phone in my room."

From then on, Coach Shoulberg would always call out to her, "Hey, Red Phone."

Coaches sometimes have some difficult decisions to make. Right away, Coach Shoulberg could see Jenny's potential and how very competitive she was, but he also saw some problems with the swim schedule. Jenny was supposed to swim both the 50-meter free and the 4 x 200-meter free relay on the same night. So he pulled Jenny aside to talk to her.

"Red Phone, I would like to see you focus on one race tonight. This could be a big night for you. I know that it would be a sacrifice, but would you consider pulling out of the relay?"

"Who would you put in my place?" Jenny asked.

"Janet Evans could do it."

"Sounds good to me, Coach. Let's concentrate on the 50."

The Dover High School student won her first international gold medal that night to become the 50 meter champion, and she got a lifetime best time. The relay team won, too.

● ● ●

Coach Parratto walked out onto the pool deck, holding his clip board with a big smile on his face. The younger team members were joking and fooling around. The older kids were quiet. They all knew what was coming.

"Seasons greetings, swimmers!" shouted the coach. "As some of you already know, today is our yearly Christmas endurance training swim. Because it is almost Christmas, and because I'm such a nice guy, I'm going to give everyone a choice. You can do a 10,000 free or sixteen 400 IMs."

"Bah,humbug," someone mumbled.

"Scrooge!" shouted one of the older boys, and several of the others joined in. "Scrooge, Scrooge, Scrooge!" Coach Parratto just smiled.

Jenny was already in the pool. "Might as well get this over with," she thought to herself, choosing to do the IMs, to avoid the boredom of swimming 10,000 meters of freestyle. It was going to be a tough workout, though. Jenny had to swim 100-meters each of the butterfly, the backstroke, the breaststroke, and the freestyle 16 times. That was over three and half miles — a total of 256 laps of the 25-meter pool.

"Sure," she thought, starting her first four pool lengths of fly, "everyone thinks that because I'm a sprinter, I only swim short distances. If they only knew!" She continued with the laps of backstroke, breaststroke and then free.

Thirteen more IMs to go!

"Coach thinks that everyone has to work on endurance, even sprinters. Isn't it enough for him," thought Jenny, "that we do dry-land training, work out in the weight room and cross-country runs?"

Nine more IMs to go!

"How about all the push-ups and sit-ups and jumping jacks and pull-ups. And those are on the easy days."

Five more IMs to go!

"On Tuesdays and Thursdays, we have two-a-days. We wake up and head for the pool while its still dark outside. We swim for an hour from 5:30 to 6:30 before school. How many days have I fallen asleep gobbling up my breakfast? And then another hour and a half after school."

Two more IMs to go!

"But Saturdays are the real killers! Every Saturday the team swims for three hours in the morning from 7 to 10 a.m. And then we swim for two more hours in the afternoon from 4 to 6 p.m.

"Friday night meets at Dover High. Early Saturday morning work-outs at Seacoast. Math homework, science reports and book reviews. Doesn't leave much time for anything else."

Jenny climbed slowly out of the pool. She flipped off her goggles and headed slowly to the locker room.

"Great swim, Jenny. You did some real good work today," said Coach Parratto.

"Thanks, Coach," said Jenny, giving a halfhearted wave, almost too tired to lift her hand.

"And Jenny... "

"Yes, Coach?"

"Merry Christmas."

"Merry Christmas, Coach. And have a happy New Year."

MARY T. MEAGHER IS KNOWN AS "MADAME BUTTERFLY" FOR WINNING THREE GOLD MEDALS IN THE 1984 LOS ANGELES OLYMPIC GAMES IN THE 100-METER BUTTERFLY, 200-METER BUTTERFLY, AND THE BUTTERFLY LEG OF THE 4 X 100-METER MEDLEY RELAY. SHE WENT ON TO WIN A SILVER AND A BRONZE

MEDAL IN THE 1988 SEOUL OLYMPIC GAMES. IN 1981 SHE SET A NEW WORLD RECORD IN THE 100 FLY, THAT HELD FOR 18 YEARS.

4

New Kid on the Block

Palo Alto, California — 1991

Jenny walked slowly through the locker room. She was carefully searching for the locker number that matched the key she had been given. It was her first day of swim practice for the Stanford University Cardinals Swim Team. Jenny was so excited. She was so nervous.

Jenny had traveled across the whole country to go to school in California. She knew that she would miss her mom and her brothers and Mike Parratto and all her friends from Dover, New Hampshire. But she also knew that she was making the right decision. Stanford was one of the best colleges in the country. Jenny wanted to study biology. She thought that someday she might want to attend medical school and become a doctor.

Stanford also had a terrific swim team. Coach Richard Quick had won college championships at both Texas and Stanford. The Cardinal women swimmers had won many medals at the Olympics.

Coach Quick had seen Jenny swim at the World Championships in Perth, Australia, the year before. Jenny had anchored the 400-meter freestyle relay, and Coach Quick had been struck by her tough competitiveness and wonderful enthusiasm. He had come twice to New Hampshire to try and convince her to come to Stanford. He offered Jenny a college scholarship to swim for the Cardinals.

So here she was at Stanford, with Lea Loveless, Janel Jorgensen and Summer Sanders.

"Hey, Jenny!" shouted one of her Stanford teammates, a swimmer she had met at Worlds last year. "Welcome to Stanford. Good Luck."

"Thanks," answered Jenny. "It's great to be here. I'll catch up with you out by the pool."

Jenny was turning the key in her lock when she felt a hand on her shoulder. She turned around and looked up.

"You're Thompson, right?" asked a very, very tall girl who stood before Jenny wearing her black swimsuit with the white "S" and her black latex swim cap with the red "S" for Stanford. "I'm one of the senior captains. I've heard some good things about you. We need a great sprinter. How ya doing?"

"Uh... great," stammered Jenny, noticing the powerful shoulders of the senior and her strong arms and legs. "Excited... and a little nervous, too."

"Well, excited is good. Nervous can be good, too, if you learn how to control it and let it work for you.

Glad to have you on the team. See you in the pool."

Jenny sat down on the bench by her locker. She had to smile to herself. "Well," she thought, "at least on this team I won't be known as Too Tall Thompson. Most of the girls are as big as I am and some seem to be a lot bigger. All of them seem strong and fit. I think that I'm going to like it here."

• • •

Jenny could barely climb out of the pool. She had never worked so hard, not even at Mike Parratto's famous Christmas swim. Coach Quick saw the look on Jenny's face and walked over.

"How was practice, Jenny? We're not working you too hard, are we now?"

What Jenny thought was, "Yes, you're killing me!" What Jenny actually said was, "No, Coach, I feel great. Practice was fun today."

The coach looked at Jenny and laughed, "You had fun today, did you? Well, I guess I've been too easy on you guys. We'll pick it up another notch at practice tomorrow."

As Coach Quick walked away, Jenny thought to herself, "Oh, no! What have I done now? What a big mouth I have!"

• • •

Jenny stuck her head in the doorway to Coach Quick's office.

Her blond hair was still wet from her after-practice shower. A thick white towel was wrapped around her neck.

"Hey, Coach, what's up? You wanted to see me?"

The coach was thumbing through the latest edition of *Swimming World* magazine. He looked up.

"I see that you are getting pretty famous and have a new nickname in all the magazines. They're calling you and Summer, Jamie Wagstaff and Nicole Haislett 'The New Kids on the Block.' Hope all this fame doesn't go to your head. How have you been feeling?"

"Real good, Coach. Good practice today."

"Do you think you're ready for our first meet tomorrow?"

"Ready, Coach. Don't worry. We'll win it for you."

"You've been doing some really good work in practice Jenny. I just wanted you to know I've got a good feeling about tomorrow and the whole season."

"Me, too, Coach. The team looks ready. I've got a good feeling, too."

Coach Richard Quick and Jenny both felt confident, and, as it turned out, with good reason. During the next four years, the Stanford Cardinals did not lose a meet and went on to win the NCAA Championships each year. All-American Jenny Thompson would win 19 NCAA titles in individual events and relays, more than any woman swimmer in college history.

• • •

Indianapolis, Indiana — March, 1, 1992

It was 45 minutes before the start of the race.

"It's just another race," Jenny assured herself. "Just like hundreds of other races I've competed in over the years."

"It's not just another race," answered a little voice inside her head. "It's the biggest, most important race ever. It's everything you've dreamed of and worked for."

Jenny took a big breath and slowly breathed the air out of her nose. "Stay relaxed and focused," she thought to herself. All around the locker room of the Indianapolis Natatorium, Jenny saw other swimmers trying to control their nervous energy.

One swimmer sat alone in the corner, her back against the wall, her knees held tightly to her chest. She was listening to a tape player, with a towel draped over her head. Another girl sat on the bench by her locker and stared down at her feet, not moving, not even blinking. One of the freestylers, who would be swimming in Jenny's heat in the prelims, was rapidly pacing back and forth, singing along to music that only she could hear and wearing nothing at all.

Jenny sat on the floor with her legs stretched out in front of her. Slowly she allowed the trunk of her body to fall forward as she reached out to touch her toes. She felt the knot in her shoulders release its tension. She grabbed her feet and pulled her toes back toward her. The muscles in her legs tightened and then relaxed.

"OK," thought Jenny, "another big breath out through the nose, stretch and relax. That's better, much better."

Jenny visited the bathroom, came back and went through more stretches. "Time to go do some warm-ups in the practice pool." She greeted some old friends. "Hey, how ya doing? Good luck today." Jenny laughed and joked with some of the other swimmers. She got out, flipped her goggles up on her head, and slipped her Stanford warm-ups on. She made her way slowly toward the other end of the competition pool.

Jenny looked up into the stands. Thousands of pairs of eyes seemed to be looking back down at her. Where was Mom? Then she spotted Mike Parratto's bushy mustache and right next to him were Mom and her brother Aaron. For just a second, Jenny smiled up at her mother and gave her a little wave.

The 100-meter freestyle was the first event on the opening day of the U.S. Olympic Trials. There was a buzz throughout the people in the stands. Only the eight fastest swimmers would be eligible to swim in the evening's finals. Only the two fastest swimmers from the night's finals would make the Olympic team.

Although Jenny had won this event at Nationals, the writers at *Swimming World* magazine did not pick her to qualify. "Well," Jenny thought, "just maybe I've got a little surprise in store."

Jenny had a little secret. No one knew. Not her teammates. Not even Mom or Aaron or Mike Parratto. The secret was that Jenny had met with Coach Quick to map out her goals for the coming year. In the space next to the 100-meter free, where Jenny was supposed to fill in the time she expected to achieve, she had written three little words: NEW WORLD RECORD. Coach Quick always said, "Before you do something, you have to believe you can do it." Jenny believed she could do it.

Jenny marched in a line with the seven other swimmers. She took her place behind her starting block. They were calling out the names of the swimmers for this heat. No more smiles. No more giggles. A look of intense concentration came over her face. Jenny's whole world had shrunk down to the size of the swimming lane in front of her. The noise of the crowd faded out. The image of Mom and Aaron and Mike Parratto disappeared. Jenny rehearsed her race in her mind. She pictured a perfect dive. She could see and feel those first few powerful strokes propelling her through the water. In her image, she got stronger and faster with each stroke. Jenny adjusted her goggles and stepped up on the block.

"Swimmers, take your mark!" called out the race official.

And they were off. Jenny had a near-perfect dive off the starting block. Right from the beginning she felt strong and sure of herself. Coming into the wall at 50 meters, she tucked her shoulder into her turn, flipped, and pushed off the wall with tremendous force. She was gaining power with each arm stroke and each kick. Something she hadn't even imagined was happening as she drove faster and faster to the finish — it felt like nothing could stop her.

Jenny made the touch and looked around for the other swimmers. As she pulled off her goggles and swim cap, Jenny heard the announcement from the public address system echoing off the walls of the Natatorium: "First Place, Jenny Thompson, of Stanford University with a time of 54.48 seconds, A NEW WORLD RECORD!"

Jenny looked over to where her mom had been sitting in the stands. Only Mom wasn't sitting any longer. Margrid Thompson, Aaron and Coach Parratto were all jumping up and down and shouting and waving their hands.

Jenny had broken the record that had belonged to the East German swimmer Kristen Otto for six years. It was the first time in 61 years that the world record for the 100-meter freestyle was held by an American woman.

That night, in the finals Jenny again finished in first place. She had officially qualified for the Olympic Games. Jenny Thompson, from Dover, New Hampshire, was going to Barcelona, Spain to represent the United States. During the medal ceremony, Jenny stood on the victory platform wearing red, white, and blue warm-ups. As the medal was placed over her head, the name "Jenny Thompson" was being written in blue paint on the wall of champions to honor her achievement. Margrid Thompson looked down at her only daughter from her place in the stands. She turned to her son Aaron and tried to speak, but no words would come. Aaron saw that there were tears of joy in his mother's eyes.

●　●　●

Barcelona, Spain — July, 1992

Zhuang Yong of the People's Republic of China and Jenny Thompson of the United States matched each other stroke for stroke as they approached the turn. It was the finals of the 100-meter freestyle. The winner would be awarded the Olympic gold medal.

As she pushed off the wall, Jenny found herself trailing the swimmer from China by inches. She drove to the wall with every ounce of her strength. She made the touch and pulled up her goggles. She turned to see the results on the big electronic scoreboard.

| Yong, Zhuang | China | 54.64 |
| Thompson, Jenny | USA | 54.84 |

As Jenny climbed out of the pool she felt both good and bad. She had missed first place by 2/10ths of one second. But she had trained hard and swum a good race. She had won the Olympic silver medal for the United States.

A sportscaster pushed in front of her blocking her path to the locker room. He shoved a microphone in front of her face.

"What went wrong?" he asked. "How does it feel to lose such an important race?"

Jenny's face turned red and her stomach twisted into a hard knot.

"I, uh... I don't know, maybe, if I..."

Jenny did not know what to say. She had swum her very best. Couldn't everyone see how hard she had tried? She wasn't a loser. She had just won the Olympic silver medal. With her head down, holding back the tears, Jenny hurried into the locker room.

The next morning in the 200-meter freestyle preliminaries, Jenny did not swim her best race. She failed to qualify for the finals. She did qualify in the 50-meter free on the last day of swimming competition. However, she only got a fifth place finish in the finals. In the Olympics only gold, silver and bronze medals are awarded to the first, second and third place finishers. "Too bad they don't give out green ribbons," Jenny laughed to herself, a little discouraged, "like when I was eight and swam for the Danvers Y."

But Jenny Thompson would not let such disappointments keep her down for long. Jenny was picked by the Olympic coaches to swim the anchor leg on the 400-meter freestyle relay. She watched from the block as her turn to swim came up. The U.S. team was a meter behind as Jenny dove in. She just would not let her teammates down. She would do whatever she had to do to win.

Jenny swam the last 100 meters split in 54.01 seconds. This was the fastest 100-meter freestyle time in history. The U.S. team won in world record time. Jenny had won her first Olympic gold medal.

For the medley relay, Jenny was again selected to swim the 100-meter freestyle anchor leg. This time, her teammates were able to give her a good lead. Jenny pulled away from the other swimmers. The U.S. team won easily. It was another world record. Jenny had won her second Olympic gold medal.

As Jenny stood on the medal platform in her red, white and blue warm-ups, the Star-Spangled Banner was played and the American flag was raised. A gold medal was hung around her neck. Jenny could think of only two things, "I feel so proud," and "I can't wait to give Mom a great big hug."

● ● ●

Dover, New Hampshire — August, 1992

Thousands of people lined Central Avenue to watch the parade. Dads lifted their kids onto their shoulders. Moms were holding their babies. Everyone was waving a red, white and blue flag.

Jenny Thompson, the gold-medal swimmer and local Olympic runners Lynn Jennings and Kathy O'Brien rode down the street in limousines. All the kids from the Seacoast Swimming Association followed along in a float. The Dover High School band played and marched along. Jenny stood up through the open roof and waved to the crowds. She wore her USA warm-ups, three shiny Olympic medals, and a wonderful smile.

It was just like the Fourth of July, except the calendar said it was August. As Jenny's limo drove past the ice-cream store, the man behind the counter dropped his ice-cream cone scooper and ran out the swinging screen door. He took off his white cap and waved to Jenny. He turned to the woman standing beside him and said, "I used to scoop ice-cream cones for Jenny and her friends every Saturday afternoon. I think my ice cream made her an Olympic swimmer."

A grandmother held tightly to the hand of her little 3-year-old granddaughter. "Karen, I've lived here, in Dover, all my life, and I've never seen anything like this. Those young ladies have made us so proud. They've made all of America proud."

"Grandma," said little Karen, squeezing her hand, "someday, I want to ride in the parade, too."

"Maybe you will, sweetheart. Maybe you will."

• • •

That fall, Jenny returned to California to Stanford University and one of the most successful and remarkable years that any competitive swimmer has ever had.

Jenny led the Stanford Cardinals to another unbeaten season, a Pac-10 Conference Championship, and another NCAA title. In the Pan Pacific Championships, Jenny set a meet record, winning an outstanding six gold medals. She won the 50-meter free, the 100-meter free, the 100-meter butterfly and three relay golds. To recognize her incredible successes, Jenny Thompson was named the U.S. Swimmer of the Year and was a finalist for the Sullivan Award and the Babe Didrikson-Zaharias Award, which honor America's greatest amateur athletes. The swimmer from the little town in New Hampshire was rewriting the record books. She was making sports history.

• • •

In the spring of 1994, everything was going so smoothly for Jenny. She had just finished a very successful junior year at Stanford, winning another NCAA championship. She was getting ready for Nationals and World Championships. She was expected to do very well in both.

It was May in California and Jenny and her friends went to a party at one of the Stanford fraternity houses. She and a friend decided to try to do a flip together on a homemade waterslide. It wasn't such a good idea for the 5-foot-6-inch , 160 pound swimmer. Jenny and her friend got entangled and landed awkwardly on each other. Jenny immediately felt a sharp pain in her arm. It was pretty bad, but she tried to ignore it. She went home and went to bed.

The pain was so bad the next morning that Jenny went to the hospital. The doctor came in with her X-ray and put it up on the light box.

"Miss Thompson, it looks like you have a very bad break in your left forearm. You must have a pretty good tolerance for pain to have waited until today to come in."

Jenny did not answer him. Her mind was busy counting the weeks until Nationals and trying to figure out how long it would take to heal.

"Miss Thompson – did you hear me?"

"Sorry," answered Jenny. "I have a very important swim meet in a few weeks, and I was wondering how long I would be out of the water."

"Miss Thompson, I don't think you understand. You have a very bad break. We will have to put a titanium plate and some screws in your arm. I am afraid you will be out of the pool for the rest of the spring and summer season."

"You don't understand, Doctor. I have to get to Nationals and place on the U.S. Team for World Championships. My coach is gonna kill me!"

The doctor continued, "I will be happy to call your coach and explain. Right now we have to make arrangements to put back together that bone in your arm."

Jenny did not panic. She knew that she was a fast healer. Besides, she loved challenges. Just how quickly could she recover? She began to see it as a new, fun challenge. And part of her would now be made of a strong, lightweight metal.

"Hey, Doc," asked Jenny, "Does titanium rust?"

A couple of days later, Jenny was in the Stanford gym working out on the exercise stair-climber to keep up her fitness level. She had a towel wrapped around her arm. Coach Quick walked by and couldn't believe what he was seeing. Jenny's optimism and confidence always amazed him.

"Jenny, what are you doing?"

"I have to keep the sweat off my arm. I can't get it wet — YET."

Two weeks later Jenny won the 100-meter freestyle at the National Championships in Indianapolis and secured a place on the team going to the World Championships.

● ● ●

Jenny first learned about tapering as a competitive swimmer in high school. As the swimming season progresses toward the big meets in the spring, the training always gets harder and harder. Because of all the miles of tough swimming workouts that they did in training over the months, the swimmers would get very tired by the time of the important competitions.

So the coaches would have their athletes taper, or reduce their swimming activity. This would give the swimmers more energy for the championship events. There is a real science to tapering before a swim meet.

The swimmers gradually reduce their heavy training and increase their rest times. The coach has to plan the tapering schedule carefully with each swimmer.

Getting enough rest is a very important part of training. When the swimmer has had the right amount of rest, she can swim faster in the championships. The coach usually plans all the hard training and tapering cycles at the beginning of the season. Sometimes the swimmers get very antsy during tapering, because they are used to more workouts, and they have a lot of extra energy. Some swimmers worry that they were not training enough to swim their best.

Jenny learned to trust her coaches. Anyway, she liked cutting back on all those long distance workouts. Because she was a sprinter, she began tapering earlier than the other swimmers. She liked the idea of getting ready for the big meets. But there were important adjustments. She had more time. She would have to make sure that she went to bed early and got enough sleep. And Jenny would have to be careful not to eat too much when she stopped training as hard.

● ● ●

Indianpolis, Indiana — April, 1996

It was 2 o'clock in the morning. The phone rang in Margrid Thompson's hotel room. She reached across the bed and picked up the receiver in the dark. She already knew who was calling.

"Mom, I'm so sorry to wake you up. I know you have to start home early tomorrow. I couldn't sleep. It seems like I haven't slept in days."

Jenny was sitting in the hallway outside her room on the other side of Indianapolis. Her back was against the wall; her knees were drawn up to her chest. The phone cord was stretched all the way out the door.

"It's all right Jenny. I was just lying here anyway. How are you doing, sweetheart?"

"Not so great, Mom. I feel like such a failure. I feel like I've let down Coach Quick and Mike Parratto and my teammates and, most of all, you."

"You didn't let anyone down, Jenny. You tried your very best. That's all anyone can ever do. And you could never let me down. I've never been so proud of you."

"Oh, Mom, it's just that everyone seems to be trying to figure out what I did wrong. They say, 'She tried too hard,' or 'She didn't try hard enough,' or 'She tapered too early,' or 'She tapered too late.' They are saying, 'Maybe she doesn't have it any more, maybe she can't win the big races.'"

"Well," said Margrid Thompson, "that's what *they* say, which isn't really that important, is it? What do *you* say, Jenny?"

"I don't know, Mom, but remember when I was 12 years old and swimming in the Junior Nationals? Well, the winner got this red, white and blue towel that said 'Junior National Champion.' And I couldn't stop thinking about how cool it would be to win that towel and bring it back to Seacoast to show the other kids. I thought about that towel so much that I couldn't think about swimming. I really messed up."

"I remember dear."

"Well, its just like that silly towel. I was swimming for all the wrong reasons. All I could think about was standing on the medal platform and winning gold medals and getting my picture in the papers. That's not why I swim."

"Go on, Jenny. I'm listening."

"Mom, I swim because I love everything about it — the training, the other girls, the traveling, the competition, moving through the water. I love being an athlete, being a swimmer. It is just so much fun. And this week, during the Olympic Trials, I forgot all that. I messed up again."

"Jenny, I know how disappointed you are that you didn't qualify in the individual events. I know how much that means to you. But you can still go to Atlanta and swim in the relays and be there for your teammates. It's up to you."

"I don't know Mom. Maybe everyone is right. Maybe I should just quit."

"Jenny, I told you a long time ago that the Thompson women are not quitters. Now, it's your decision — you can go on to the Olympics in Atlanta and swim in the relays, or you can stay home and watch your friends on television and feel sorry for yourself. It's your choice. Don't let anyone else make it for you!"

"I don't know... maybe you're right. I'll think about it. Thanks, Mom."

"Jenny, just remember — everyone's life has disappointments. If life were all perfect — it would be boring. Whatever you decide to do, I will always be proud of you, and I will always love you, no matter what."

"I know, Mom. Thanks. Goodnight."

"Goodnight, Jenny."

Margrid Thompson lay in bed and stared up at the ceiling of her hotel room for quite a while. Finally, a dull light began to creep in under the window shades. Across town, her daughter was sleeping soundly and peacefully for the first time in many days. It was the sleep of someone who had already made up her mind.

JANET EVANS SWAM IN THREE OLYMPIC GAMES: 1988, 1992 AND 1996. SHE WON FOUR GOLD MEDALS AND ONE SILVER MEDAL. HER SPECIALTY WAS DISTANCE SWIMMING — THE 400-METER, 800-METER AND 1500-METER FREESTYLE EVENTS. SHE HAS A SWIM MEET NAMED IN HER HONOR: THE JANET EVANS INVITATIONAL IN LOS ANGELES. AT THE OPENING CEREMONIES OF THE 1996 GAMES IN ATLANTA, JANET EVANS WAS GIVEN THE THRILLING DISTINCTION OF BEING THE LAST OLYMPIC TORCH RUNNER — HANDING IT TO MUHAMMAD ALI.

CHAMPIONS *of the* WATER

5

Gold Rush

Ladies and gentlemen, please bring your seat to its full upright position. Stow your carry-on bags under your seats. Turn off any personal electronic equipment. Buckle your seat-belts. Prepare for takeoff.

Jenny shoved her carry-on gym bag underneath the seat in front of her. Inside the bag were a few Atlanta '96 T-shirts she bought to give to her friends, her goggles, the Team USA swim cap with her name on it, an anatomy text book, her portable CD player and a couple of CD's, some gum, a comb, spare sunglasses and three Olympic gold medals.

Although Jenny had not qualified to swim in any of the individual events, she was a very important part of the U.S. swim team. Because of her experience and enthusiasm, her teammates looked to Jenny as the unofficial team cheerleader. Jenny swam the very important anchor leg in both the 4 x 100 and 4 x 200 freestyle relays. Jenny wore a huge smile as she stood, once again, on the victory platform with her teammates. All four swimmers were wearing gold medals around their necks. The U.S. flag was raised, and the national anthem was played. Jenny also swam in the preliminaries of the medley relay race. The U.S. team won the gold in the finals of that race, too. It was fun to swim as a team in the relay events and share the glory with her teammates.

The airplane turned toward the west as it gained altitude and flew higher and higher. Jenny looked out the window and saw the red clay of the Georgia flatlands as far as the eye could see. Jenny remembered the curious look the TV announcer had given her after her last race.

"Well, Jenny, now that your swimming career is over, what will you be doing?"

"Hey," Jenny had answered, looking him straight in the eye, "who says my swimming career is over? I just might have a few surprises left in me yet."

Jenny thought back to her days swimming for the Danvers Dolphins. She remembered learning the butterfly stroke and practicing day after day after day. She remembered setting a district record in her very first race.

"Hm," thought Jenny, "it's like Coach Quick always says — the first step toward doing something is believing you can do it." Could she be the one to break one of the longest-standing, most admired records in all of competitive swimming? Mary T. Meagher had set the world record in the 100-meter butterfly 15 years before.

"Well, I think I have the talent, and I know I have

the determination. With Coach Quick's help and enough tough training, I might just be able to do it. In fact, I know I can."

Jenny closed her eyes as the plane headed toward California and the setting sun.

• • •

No matter how many years Jenny had been training for competitive swimming, she would never get used to waking up at 5:15 a.m. It was never easy. It helped that she was now determined to reach a big goal — to break the record in the 100-meter butterfly.

It was still dark outside at the Stanford 50-meter pool. Coach Quick already had the day's workout scribbled on the training board. Jenny went over with her cup of coffee to see what the day's torture would be. A 1000-meter warm-up and then a few thousand meters alternating between a fast pace and a medium pace. "Do-able," thought Jenny to herself.

By 8:30 a.m., Jenny was already in the weight room, working with the athletic trainer. Each day's strength-training was different. Today, it was lower-body conditioning with heavy weights. As she pushed and breathed and lifted, she thought of how it would make her kicks stronger in the water.

Noon. Time for lunch. Today she was staying on campus to hang out with some former teammates

and join in a campus yoga class at 1:15. At 2:30 p.m., she was in the gym, on a stationary bicycle, participating in a "spinning" class to fast-paced music.

She had been doing a routine like this for many years — more years than she had dreamed of. Two Olympics had come and gone. Some people were starting to ask her about the 2000 Olympics in Sydney, Australia. She couldn't think about that yet — she was focusing on that 100 fly record. The time of 57.93 seconds had stood since 1981.

At 3:30 in the afternoon, it was back to the pool for water circuit training. It was Coach Quick's special strength and power workout. There were four stations set up in the water. At each station, Jenny and three other swimmers would train for 20 minutes and then switch when Coach Quick blew the whistle. At the first station, Jenny had to swim as fast as she could while towing a mesh equipment bag. Next, at the power kick station, Jenny had to do vertical-kicking while holding a 10-pound weight. Then, Jenny practiced mid-pool power turns. Finally, the swimmers dove in with 25 feet of surgical tubing tied around their waists. Jenny swam as hard as she could while the rubber band tubing was pulling her back to the start. This kind of workout was fun — but tough.

"Ah," thought Jenny, "Dinnertime." And boy was she hungry! Hopefully, tonight she would be able to finish the mystery novel she was reading. After all, it would then be only a few hours until the next practice day.

•••

Sydney, Australia — August 24, 1999

"Australia is like swimming heaven," Jenny thought to herself as she began her stretches. It was 45 minutes before the start of the 100-meter butterfly finals. "The Australians just love swimmers and cheer them as much as basketball players and football players get cheered back in the U.S. I know the crowds will be cheering for their own Susie O'Neil; I'll just pretend that the cheers are for me."

Jenny was in Sydney to compete in the 1999 Pan-Pacific Championships. The meet was being held at the Olympic Pool at Homebush Bay, where the swimming races for the 2000 Olympics would be next summer. She was in great shape, and she was ready for a fantastic meet.

Jenny had already won a first place gold medal in the 100-meter freestyle. Could she also win the 100 fly? She was getting close to Mary T. Meagher's 18-year old record time. Could she set a new world record? Anything was a possibility to Jenny.

Just a few weeks earlier in the USA Swimming National Championships, Jenny had swum the second fastest 100-meter butterfly of all time — just 2/10ths of a second off the record. "It's more like a mental barrier than a physical barrier." Jenny tried to reach inside herself to find the strength to break through this "mental barrier."

As an 11-year-old, Jenny had first watched Mary T. Meagher on TV during the Los Angeles Olympics in 1984. Now, as part of her preparation, she had studied the stroke of her childhood hero on a swimming website on the internet. Jenny felt the positive energy through the computer screen. She watched her hero in action again and again. She knew that every single movement — every arm-pull, breath and kick had to be perfect. It could make the difference of a fraction of a second.

At her starting block, Jenny waited for the formal introductions of the swimmers. She felt peaceful and calm. "Funny," she thought, "I really didn't feel that great yesterday or this morning. But right now, at this very moment, I feel absolutely ready."

There was a murmur in the stands. Jenny smiled as she saw some American fans unfurl a giant red, white and blue U.S. flag, the width of an entire spectator section. Jenny took a deep breath and adjusted her goggles. She stepped up on the starting block, looking up and giving a little wave to her mom seated in the stands.

"Swimmers, take your marks."

Jenny's strong arms and powerful shoulders propelled her through the water. She felt just right. She was swimming the race of her life. Yet, as she made the turn and pushed off toward the finish, Jenny saw Australia's Susie O'Neil in the next lane matching her stroke for stroke. Twenty-five meters to go. Fifteen thousand people were on their feet, cheering wildly. Ten meters to go. Jenny dug down deep. She had to reach inside for everything she had to give. The wall was coming up. The finish.

• • •

Dover, New Hampshire — several time zones away

The kids were so excited as they waited by the pool for their coach to come out.

"This is how I swim the butterfly!" shouted one boy gesturing with his arms.

"No, that's not right," his friend called over, "Here, watch me! This is how Jenny Thompson does it."

Coach Parratto walked outside, wearing his Seacoast Swimming Association cap and T-shirt. He had a huge smile under his bushy mustache.

"Well, I guess you've all heard the news. . . Jenny Thompson just swam the 100 Fly in 57.88 — a new World Record. She broke a record that was held for 18 years. Our Jenny is still making swimming history! What do you say we go and have a great practice in honor of Jenny's new record?"

"I know what Jenny would tell us if she were here," said Karen. "'Don't forget to have fun!'"

"You're absolutely right," answered Coach

Parratto. "I think that's exactly what Jenny Thompson would say.

•   •   •

Sydney, Australia — August 25, 1999

Rubbing the sleep from her eyes, Jenny Thompson opened the door of her hotel room. She wore a fluffy white robe and held a steaming mug of coffee. As she picked up the *Sydney Morning Herald* from outside her door, she glanced at the day's headline:

WONDER WOMAN is The New Madame Butterfly!

•   •   •

>**Chat Host**: Let me introduce our special guest for the Golden Stars of the Pool chat session. Jenny Thompson made history last August when she broke the world record in the 100-meter butterfly, held for 18 years. She has won five Olympic gold medals. She has been part of four NCAA championship teams at Stanford. Jenny is currently training for the 2000 Olympic Trials.

>**Mike C. of Long Meadow, MA** : How many hours a day do you train?

>**JENNY**: I usually train about 6–7 hours a day. That includes about two hours of swimming in the morn-

ing, an hour of weight training or Pilates, some yoga, an hour of stretching, spinning classes and two hours of swimming in the afternoon. That's why "eau de chlorine" is my perfume. It is pretty much a full-time job — only without the pay!

>**Sarah S. of La Jolla, CA**: What accomplishment are you most proud of?

>**JENNY:** I've broken world records and medaled in two Olympics through hard work and a love of swimming. I even have a pool named after me in my hometown. But right now I am most proud of being accepted to medical school. That is a big dream come true, too.

>**J.S. of Philadelphia:** Do you think "shaving down" helps you swim faster?

>**JENNY**: Yes, I sure do! It's kind of a tradition in my sport. Everybody waits until right before a big meet and then shaves their arms and legs — guys even do their chests. It is a ritual that most swimmers like to do together. I even let the hair grow under my arms until I shave down before a big meet.

>**Alice C. of New York City:** Do you eat anything special that makes you so fast?

>**JENNY**: Ben & Jerry's Chunky Monkey ice cream is my secret weapon. No, just kidding. I do love it, but I do not eat it that often. I really pay attention to

eating nutritious meals. I eat lots of small meals that will give me a high energy level. I also drink lots of water all day.

>**Emmett D. of New Jersey**: How do you deal with disappointments in competition?

>**JENNY:** There are always disappointments — its part of the game. I try and use them — to learn from them for the next time. It motivates me for the next swim. It's how I get better and better. Swimming has taught me to love challenges. And I will stay away from negative people, too. It's important to stay positive and keep it fun.

>**Janey G. of Rhinebeck, NY:** You are one of my heroes. Who are your heroes?

>**JENNY**: In swimming, there are several women who have inspired me. Dawn Fraser of Australia, Tracey Caulkins and, of course, Mary T. Meagher. I found Wonder Woman to be a great role model of courage and power. But my greatest hero is my mom. She has been the best role model for me. She is so strong and smart, and she has taught me what determination really means.

>**Chat Host:** Thank you, Jenny Thompson. That's all the time we have tonight. Next week in the Golden Stars of the Pool chat room, Lenny Krayzelburg.

● ● ●

Sydney, Australia — September 16, 2000

Jenny powered her way to the finish. She was swimming the anchor leg of the 4 x 100 meter freestyle relay final. Jenny made the turn and took a big lead. There were less than 50 meters to go. Less than 50 meters to an incredible sixth Olympic gold medal.

Jenny's three teammates were jumping up and down, waving their hands and shouting insanely. Amy Van Dyken, Dara Torres and Courtney Shealy cheered Jenny to victory.

"Go Jenny!"

"Come on, kid, you can do it!"

"Yes, Jenny! Yes! Yes! Yes!"

Jenny made the touch. She ripped off her cap and goggles. All four swimmers turned to the giant scoreboard.

1.	USA 3 min. 36.61 sec.	WR

"Ladies and gentlemen," echoed the public address announcer, over the thousands of cheering people at the Sydney Olympic Pool, "A new world and Olympic record!"

On the victory platform, Amy sobbed uncontrollably. She had come back from two shoulder operations after winning four gold medals in 1996. Dara's eyes filled with tears. At age 33, she had returned to swimming after a seven-year retirement. Jenny just smiled and waved. She was so happy and proud. It was all a wonderful dream come true.

• • •

Jenny went on to win two more gold medals at the Sydney Olympics. She swam the last leg of the 4 x 200-meter freestyle relay. The U.S. women came in first place and set a new Olympic record. Three days later, Jenny swam the butterfly in the 4x100 medley relay. Again, the U.S. women came in first place. It was another world record.

Jenny Thompson had represented the United States in three different Olympics — in Barcelona in 1992, in Atlanta in 1996, and in Sydney in 2000. She had won a total of 10 Olympic medals, and eight of the medals were gold. She had won more medals than any other female swimmer in the world. She had won more Olympic gold medals than any other American female athlete, ever.

Jenny never did win a gold in an individual event in the Olympics. Her last chance in the 2000 Olympics was in the 100-meter freestyle event. Incredibly, both she and her teammate Dara Torres finished in exactly the same time. They tied for third place, and each won a bronze medal.

After the race, Jenny and Margrid Thompson hugged by the victory stand. They were laughing

and crying at the same time.

"Jenny, I'm so proud of you. We all are. I hope you appreciate what an amazing person you are. You're not disappointed about the 100-meter free, are you?"

"No, Mom. It's time for me to stop looking at what I don't have and start looking at what I do have."

"Jenny, you are a real life hero for thousands of American kids."

"And you are my hero, Mom. You always have been, and you always will be."

"Oh, Jenny. Do you remember those kids who used to call you Too Tall Thompson and all those other nasty names?"

"Yeah, I sure do, Mom. Why do you ask?"

"Well," said Margird Thompson, "now all they will call you is Olympic champion."

Jenny Thompson was named Athlete of the Year by the Women's Sports Foundation for her incredible performances in Sydney and throughout her long and successful swimming career. She has enrolled at the Columbia University School of Medicine.

Jenny Thompson's Career Highlights

It all started in 1987 – when Jenny Thompson won the Rookie of the Meet Award at Spring Nationals. It was the beginning of 14 years as a member of the USA Swimming's National A Team. Among her numerous championships and awards:

- ◆ 10 Olympic medals:
  8 Gold, 1 Silver, 1 Bronze
  - 1992 (Barcelona): second 100 free; first 400 free relay; first 400 medley relay
  - 1996 (Atlanta): first 400 free relay; first 800 free relay; first 400 medley relay
  - 2000 (Sydney): first 400 free relay; first 800 free relay; first 400 medley relay; third 100 fly
- ◆ World records in the 100 free, 50 free and 100 fly
- ◆ American records in the 100 free and 100 fly
- ◆ 23 U.S. National Titles
- ◆ 22 Pan-Pacific Championship Titles — 1989–1999
- ◆ Seven-time NCAA Individual Champion

- 1992, 1998, 1999 — Phillips Performance Award
- 1993, 1998 — USS Swimmer of the Year
- 1993, 1997 — Robert J.H. Kiputh Award
- 1995 — Honda-Broderick Sport Award (outstanding college swimmer)
- 1998 — Henry P. Iba Citizenship Award
- 1998 — World Swimmer of the Year, *Swimming World*
- 1999 — USOC Sportswoman of the Year
- 1999 — USS performance of the Year
- 1999 — Named as one of the Top 100 Female Athletes of the Century, *Sports Illustarted*
- 2000 — named to the New England Women's Sports Hall of Fame
- 2000 — Women's Sports Foundation Athlete of the Year Award

Sports Talk

To Parents, Teachers, and Coaches:

In this section you will see a discussion of some of the issues presented by Jenny's story as a young female athlete. We also share with you some information about the influence of sports participation on girls, and we have suggested some discussion questions for you. We encourage you to talk about these topics with the young reader. Starting a dialogue and exchanging ideas can enhance this story for the soon-to-be athlete and make the sports experience more enjoyable for the young, accomplished athlete.

Dealing with Disappointments

Jenny has been described by her coaches as a very dedicated and highly competitive athlete. They meant it as a compliment. Her perseverance helped her to pursue her goals and dreams. Sure, she was determined to win and help her team win, but more than that, she had personal goals to achieve. She wanted to perfect her skills, to swim her own best possible times and to keep having fun. Jenny has also had some big disappointments in her athletic career. But she is the first to say that she has accomplished much more than she ever imagined. She is very proud of herself. This is a great life lesson.

Sports can be a valuable learning environment for life. With its wins and losses and ups and downs and ups again — it can show kids how to stick with something. The emphasis of sports should be on the inner rewards of competition, such as learning how to make decisions, leadership training, meeting challenges and working with others. Competitive sports can teach girls to be strategic, to plan ahead, to relax under stress, to concentrate and stay focused. Training for and competing in sports requires a commitment. From this commitment of time and effort, a young girl learns how to set goals, take responsibility and prepare for the challenges of life. She has the opportunity to learn how to accept failure and be a gracious winner while enjoying the thrill of success.

Q: Jenny loved to swim and she really loved to compete. How does it feel to win? How does it feel to lose? Do you think that losing would make Jenny stop swimming?

Body Image

Jenny was much stronger and more muscular than the other girls in school. She also had to wear an awkward back brace for her scoliosis. She was teased and called names. For a while it really upset her when the other kids teased her. Youngsters become aware of being big or little, fat or thin at a very early age. Both boys and girls can have distorted self-images about what they should look like. A lot of that has to do with the images they see in magazines and on television. Most girls are uncomfortable with what they look like. Most think, incorrectly, that they are too big or overweight.

Jenny gained a lot of confidence from being a great athlete. Along with this, she began to feel more secure about how healthy and powerful her body was. She realized when she met other elite female swimmers that this is what athletes can look like. Girls are generally more negative about their bodies than boys. Girls can learn through sport to view their bodies in a positive way. Swimming really helped Jenny to have a strong and healthy body image.

Jenny has become a wonderful role model for all girls, and especially for young female athletes everywhere. Sixteen-year-old Megan Quann, Olympic medalist in the 2000 Olympics said upon seeing Jenny Thompson for the first time at a meet, "Oh my God, there's one of my heroes — and look at those shoulders!"

Q: Think of different sports — gymnastics, shot put, pole vault, weightlifting, figureskating. What would your body have to look like to do well in these sports? What part of your body do you like the best?

Competitive Anxiety

Athletes at all levels feel pressure. It can come from their coaches, their teammates, their parents and especially from themselves. Everyone wants to succeed. It depends what is taught to the young athlete. Is it the fun of playing the sport and learning new things and being with teammates? Or is it all about winning?

Jenny felt very nervous at times, especially as a young swimmer. It even made her too nervous to eat on meet days. As she got older, she learned to use her nervous energy. But even Jenny was affected by the importance and pressures of some big swim meets. Being a little nervous can sometimes be good, too. Everyone feels excited before competition. It can be energizing, as Jenny says, "If you learn how to control it and let it work for you."

There are some hazards to placing a child in an overly competitive environment. It should be age-appropriate. It should be either stress-free, or, the young person should be taught anxiety-reducing skills. There should be lots of positive feedback. Help the young athlete to find something good about each difficult practice and competition. Remember to keep it fun — the most important element of youth sports.

Q: What happens to you when you get nervous? What happened to Jenny? What could you do to calm down?

The Benefits of Sports Participation for Girls

More than ever before, American girls are actively involved in sports. Recent research has demonstrated the importance and value of exercise and sports for girls. These lessons learned in childhood help to shape the developing adult. Sports influence girls' physical health, psychological well-being, overall social development and academic achievement.

Girls have a difficult time these days. Many have overwhelming concerns about their competence, self-worth and body image. Regular participation in exercise and sports programs provides tangible experiences of achievement that teach girls problem-solving skills and promote self-confidence. Through the influence of healthy role models and interaction with teammates, young athletes learn how to deal with failure and how to create expectations of success.

Involvement in sports and the development of an identity as an athlete helps a young girl to get through the everyday stresses by increasing self-esteem, lowering tension and teaching her how to better handle challenges. Being physically active helps to create a healthy body image. Being an athlete also encourages girls to avoid risky actions and learn responsible social behaviors. It can also be an antidote to such social problems as teen pregnancy, substance abuse and violent behaviors.

Sports are an educational asset in girls' lives. Research findings show that high school female athletes report higher grades and lower drop-out rates and are more likely to go on to college than their non-athlete counterparts. Team sports and the competitive arena are a natural place to learn the lessons of positive conflict resolution. The universal character of sport helps to break down barriers, challenge stereotypes and act as a tool for tolerance.

General discussion questions:

What do you think makes playing sports fun?

Who are your heroes in sports?

What makes her/him special?

What do you need to be good at sports?

How do you get ready to play your sport?

What do you worry about when you play sports?

What is the most important part of playing your sport?

How important is winning? Would you do anything to win?

What happens when you lose?

Women's Swimming

Swimming has long been one of the most popular sports for girls in the United States. There are many opportunities for competitive and recreational swimming. There are community programs, the YMCA, private clubs and school swim teams.

PROGRAMS:

USA Swimming is the national governing body for men's and women's swimming in the United States. The various national and international competitions are:

The Olympic Games (the highest level of swimming)
World Championships
Pan-Pacific Championships
Pan American Games
Goodwill Games
U.S. Open Championships
NCAA Championships
Senior Nationals
Junior Nationals
Regional & district events
Competitive invitational events

125

RESOURCES:

Resources for girls and women's sports and fitness information:

The Women's Sports Foundation:
www.womensportsfoundation.org

Just Sports for Women:
www.SportsforWomen.com

The Melponeme Institute:
www.melponeme.org

GirlPower!Sports & Fitness:
www.health.org/gpower

Resources for Swimming Information:

United States Olympic Committee:
www.usoc.org/sports

The USOC now has an area on their website called "Where do I Play?"-that will list clubs for sports in your area.

United States Swimming Association:
www.usa-swimming.org
The governing body for swimming in the United States

Federation Internationale de Natation Amateur (FINA):
www.fina.org
International governing body for amateur competitve swimming

International Olympic Committee:
www.olympic.org

International Swimming Hall of Fame:
www.isof.org

Swimming News Online:
www.swimnews.com

Swimming information:
www.swiminfo.com

American Swimming Coaches Association (ASCA):
301 SE 20th Street
Fort Lauderdale, FL 33316
305/462-6267

Books:

The Young Swimmer By Jeff Rouse
DK Publishing, New York, NY (1997)
Sports Illustrated Competitive Swimming techniques for Champions By Mark Schubert
Winners Circle Books, New York, NY (1996)
Swimming Into the 21st Century By Cecil M. Colwin
Human Kinetics, Champaign, IL (1992)

A Brief History of USA Women's Swimming

American women have been very successful in swimming for a very long time. There are so many great females in USA swimming history. We have highlighted one special champion at the beginning of each chapter. We will mention a few more here. For more information, consult the Resources section.

Ethelda Bleibtrey was the first American woman to win an Olympic swimming title and the first woman from any country to win three gold medals. She won her golds in freestyle events at the 1920 Olympics.

Eleanor Holm won 29 National Championships. She held six world records in the backstroke. She won a gold medal in the 1932 Olympic Games in Los Angeles.

Debbie Meyer was the first woman to win three individual gold medals in a single Olympics in 1968 in Mexico City.

Shirley Babashoff won eight Olympics medals in the 1972 and 1976 Olympics. Her achievements were in freestyle events.

Tracey Caulkins is considered by some to be the greatest all-around swimmer of all time. She is the only swimmer, ever, to own American records in every stroke — freestyle, backstroke, breaststroke, and butterfly. She won three gold medals at the 1984 Olympics in Los Angeles.

• • •

Individual Event Highlights at the Olympic Level
Most of the swimming events were not held for women until 1964, but USA women have been winning medals since the 1920 Olympics.

1920: USA women swept the 100 and 400 freestyle events.

1924: USA women swept the 100 and 400 freestyle events; gold and bronze in the 100 backstroke; silver in the 200 breaststroke.

1928: USA women won the gold and silver in the 100 freestyle; gold in the 400 freestyle.

1932: USA women won gold and bronze in the 100 freestyle; gold and silver in the 400 freestyle; gold in the 100 backstroke.

1936: USA women won bronze in the 400 freestyle; bronze in the 100 backstroke.

1948: USA women won gold in the 400 freestyle; silver in the 100 freestyle.

1952: USA women won bronze in the 400 freestyle.

1956: USA women swept the 100 butterfly; silver in the 100 backstroke; bronze in the 400 freestyle.

1960: USA women won the gold in the 400 freestyle; gold in the 100 butterfly; gold in the 100 backstroke.

1964: USA women swept the 400 freestyle; swept the 400 individual medley; silver and bronze in the 100 freestyle; gold and bronze in the 100 backstroke; silver in the 200 breaststroke; gold and bronze in the 100 butterfly.

1968: USA women swept the 100 freestyle; swept the 200 freestyle; gold and silver in the 400 freestyle; gold in the 800 freestyle; swept the 200 individual medley event; gold and bronze in the 100 backstroke; bronze in the 200 backstroke; gold in the 200 breaststroke; bronze in the 100 breaststroke; silver and bronze in the 100 butterfly; bronze in the 200 butterfly; gold and silver in the 400 individual medley.

1972: USA women swept the 200 butterfly; won gold and silver in the 100 freestyle; gold and silver in the 200 backstroke; gold in the 100 breaststroke; gold and bronze in the 100 backstroke; silver and bronze in the 200 freestyle; silver in the 200 breaststroke; bronze in the 200 individual medley.

1976: USA women won silver in the 200 freestyle; silver in the 400 freestyle; silver and bronze in the 800 freestyle; bronze in the 100 butterfly.

1984: USA female swimmers tied for the gold in the 100 freestyle; gold and silver in the 200 individual medley event; gold and silver in the 200 freestyle; gold in the 400 freestyle; gold and silver in the 800 freestyle; gold in the 400 individual medley; gold and silver in the 100 backstroke; silver in the 200 backstroke; silver in the 200 breaststroke; gold in the 200 butterfly; gold and silver in the 100 butterfly.

1988: USA female swimmers won gold in the 400 freestyle; gold in the 800 freestyle; gold in the 400 individual medley; bronze in the 50 freestyle; bronze in the 200 butterfly.

1992: USA female swimmers won gold in the 200 freestyle; gold in the 800 freestyle; gold in the 200 butterfly; silver in the 200 individual medley; silver in the 100 butterfly; silver in the 100 breaststroke; bronze in the 400 individual medley; silver in the 400 freestyle; bronze in the 50 freestyle; bronze in the 200 breaststroke; bronze in the 100 backstroke.

1996: USA females won gold in the 50 freestyle; gold in the 800 freestyle; gold and silver in the 100 backstroke; bronze in the 100 freestyle; silver in the 200 backstroke; silver in the 100 breaststroke; silver in the 200 breaststroke; gold and bronze in the 100 butterfly; silver in the 400 individual medal.

2000: USA women won the gold in the 100 breast-stroke; gold in the 200 butterfly; gold and silver in the 800 freestyle; silver in the 200 breaststroke; bronze in the 400 individual medley; bronze in the 200 breaststroke; bronze in the 100 freestyle; bronze in the 100 butterfly; bronze in the 50 freestyle.

Glossary

Altitude: the height above the earth's surface

Amateur: a person who is not a professional; a person who does not get paid

Anchor: the anchor leg is the last swimmer in the relay

Asthma: an illness with attacks of wheezing, coughing and hard breathing

Biology: the science of living things (plants and animals)

Block: the starting platform where the swimmer dives into the pool to begin his/her race

Butterfly: swimming stroke in which the arms do an overhead motion together and the legs do a dolphin kick

Challenged: questioned

Circuit Training: training for a sport by going from one exercise station to another

Dolphin Kick: an up and down leg kick used during butterfly

Dry-Land Training: strength training exercises out of the pool

Eligible: being qualified; having met the required conditions

Endurance: to perform over a long time or long distance

Experience: something that a person has done or lived through

Federal Style: colonial building style, noted for red brick

Final: the final race of an event that decides the winner

Freestyle: swim stroke also called the "crawl" with alternate overhead motion of the arms and a flutter kick

Frustrated: kept from getting what one wants

Geography: the study of the places on earth

Gesturing: expressing an idea or feeling with hands and arms

Guinea Pig: a person that is used in an experiment

Gradually: slowly; little by little

Heat: race in which swimmers try to get the fastest times to qualify for the final championship race

Ignition: the electrical system that starts the engine of the car

Individual Medley (IM): an event in which the swimmer uses all four competitive strokes; butterfly, backstroke, breaststroke, freestyle

Medley Relay (MR): an event in which a team of four swimmers each swim one of the four different strokes: backstroke, breaststroke, butterfly, freestyle.

Muffled: quiet, unclear sounds
Official: a judge on the deck of the pool
Patriotic: showing great love for one's country
Pediatrician: a doctor who takes care of children
Preliminaries (prelims): races in which swimmers try to qualify for the finals
Prestigious: famous; honored
Propelled: driven forward; pushed
Rehearsal: a practice for a performance
Ritual: a set thing to do
Rival: competitor
Sarcastically: saying in a mocking, funny way
Spectator: a person who is watching some event
Split: the individual swimmer's time in a race
Sprinter: someone who races fast, short distances
Stopwatch: a watch that can be started and stopped to measure the time of a race in fractions of a second
Taper: the resting process in training for competition
Temporary: lasting only for a short time
Titanium: a very light, strong metal
Tolerance: ability to put up with something painful or unpleasant
Touch: the finish of the race
Tradition: a custom that is handed down
Triceps: the muscles at the back of the upper arm
Trudged: walked with a lot of effort
Unfurl: to unroll, spread out

Vibrant: lively

Yoga: form of exercise that includes stretching and
breathing

About the Authors

Dr. Doreen Greenberg is a certified consultant in sport psychology and has worked with school, college, professional and Olympic athletes from a variety of sports. These experiences have ranged from consulting with national and world champions to helping young children with their initial fears about training and competition. Dr. Greenberg was a primary author of *Physical Activity and Sport in the Lives of Girls* (1997), a report for the President's Council on Physical Fitness and Sports; an associate editor of *The Encyclopedia of Women and Sport in America* (Oryx Press, 1998), and editor of *Sport in the Lives of Urban Girls* (Women's Sports Foundation, 1998).

Michael A. Greenberg is a former English teacher and retired business executive. While going to college in the Boston area in the late 1960's, he attended every Sixers-Celtics game at the old Boston Garden. Unfortunately, he was supposed to be attending classes at the time.

Michael and Doreen have two grown daughters and live at the New Jersey shore with their three dogs.

Did You Enjoy This Book?

Be sure to look for other titles in the *Anything You Can Do ...* series:

A Drive to Win: The Story of Nancy Lieberman-Cline
(isbn: 1-930546-40-8)

Sword of a Champion: The Story of Sharon Monplaisir
(isbn: 1-930546-39-4)

Fast Lane to Victory: The Story of Jenny Thompson
(isbn: 1-930546-38-6)

For information about these and other quality
Wish Publishing titles, check out our website:
www.wishpublishing.com

CPSIA information can be obtained at www.ICGtesting.com
Printed in the USA
BVOW02s1440080414

350077BV00001B/16/A